"I love *The Speaker's Toolbox*. This book is an excellent resource for building an award-winning speech and a great reference source for those who aspire to be great speakers, both neophytes and vets."

Kenny Ray Morgan, Two Time World Champion Finalist

"Brian Woolf got it right! He covers all the essentials in his book, *The Speaker's Toolbox*. If you want to be a powerful presenter, this book is full of ideas to help you. I wish this resource was around when I started. Well done!"

Darren LaCroix, CSP, AS, World Champion Speaker

"This book will be of immense help to anyone in any walk of life where communication is a part of his or her job. After decades of listening to presentations by senior executives of big companies, I just wish that some of them had read this first!"

Robin Clark, Co-Founder, The Wise Marketer

"Brian—Tremendous research! You clearly do have a passion for speeches. You've provided a book that will teach many for years to come!"

Harold Patterson, World Champion Speaker

"*The Speaker's Toolbox* is fascinating and I'd think would be very helpful to all kinds of folk. The tone is quite inviting. I love the specific examples of various points such as the twists. Were I still teaching there is much I would like to use!"

Malinda Tulloh, Ph.D., Professor of English (Retired)

"Let me express how impressed I am with your book. Great job! The useful tools you've included and the numerous speeches you've analyzed will be a blessing for every speaker."

Presiyan Vasilev, World Champion Speaker

"Thank you so much Brian! I received rave reviews about your presentations on your book."

Kimberley Love, District Director, D58, Toastmasters International®

"I will require every one of my protégés to read this book. It lays out so succinctly the key elements that so many speakers struggle with, the things that are so hard to explain. I loved the combination of great minds and speakers outside Toastmasters as well as those within. The footnoting procedure is excellent. Thank you for writing this excellent book!"

Randy J. Harvey, World Champion Speaker

"I had the opportunity to meet and hear Brian Woolf, author of *The Speaker's Toolbox*. He is an amazing speaker and teacher. I highly recommend this book!"

Ray Ciafardini, Jr., Toastmaster

THE SPEAKER'S TOOLBOX

47 Tools to Build Better Speeches

BRIAN WOOLF

The Speaker's Toolbox: 47 Tools to Build Better Speeches

ISBN-13: 978-09632025-7-4

Library of Congress Control Number: 2016944774

1. Speech. 2. Public Speaking 3. Communications

1701

Cover Design: Amy Tedder, *www.atyourdesign.com*

Published by Teal Books
In conjunction with:
Fiction Addiction Publishing Services
1175 Woods Crossing Rd., #5
Greenville, S.C. 29607
864-675-0540
www.fiction-addiction.com
www.fpspublishing.com

To order additional copies, please visit:

www.amazon.com
www.fiction-addiction.com

For quantity discounts, please contact the author at:
brianwoolf@speakers-toolbox.com

Dedication

To all the World Champions of Public Speaking,
winners of Toastmasters® annual prestigious award
who through their example have
raised the level of speaking excellence globally,
and who have openly and generously
helped so many others
improve their communication skills.

Special Thanks

My special thanks to Randy Harvey, the 2004 World
Champion, friend and mentor, who introduced me to so
many new paths to understand communication, including
Radio Commentary and Varying Your Visual Speaking
Height, two tools in this book. It has been a remarkably
enriching and enjoyable education.

Contents

Contents

Introduction

This book is written for newer speakers: those closer to the bottom than the top of Speech Mountain. By emphasizing the three critical elements of speaking—A Clear Message, Close Audience Connection, and Helping Your Audience Remember—you learn to speak better...faster.

A set of tools is offered to help you achieve this goal: tools drawn from the practices of speakers across continents and centuries. Each tool, after being explained, is followed by numerous examples from actual speeches showing how the tool was used. It is my experience that one learns best and quickest by seeing an example, then adapting and doing likewise.

Just as every craftsman uses different tools as he works on different jobs, so too speakers choose different tools as they give different speeches to different audiences. The tools in this book comprise many that you will need as you construct those speeches.

Arranged alphabetically for easy reference, each tool covers two pages. To use this Toolbox effectively, quickly scan the tools and select those that you would like to get comfortable with first. Then, when preparing your next speech, make a conscious effort to use at least one of them. Keep repeating the process with these and other tools. Over time, you will find yourself building better speeches as you find yourself automatically applying the diverse tools you have uncovered.

To highlight best speaking practices more than best speaking practitioners, the pages are filled with best practices while the names of the best practitioners are shown in the book's Back Notes via superscripts, eg, in the tool Alliteration [79-3] refers to Ted Mathew and [JFK] refers to John F Kennedy.

Some examples, unsurprisingly, are not unique to one tool. Accordingly, you will see some examples appear several times in the Toolbox.

As this book is aimed at newer rather than seasoned speakers it favors simplicity. For example, technical, hard-to-pronounce, rhetorical terms have been omitted—on the assumption that your primary interest is in becoming a better speaker, not an academic.

The book closes with 11 world-class speeches that demonstrate many of the tools you are now about to discover. Enjoy and learn.

With best wishes on your journey up Speech Mountain ...

Brian Woolf
Greenville, S.C.
July 10, 2016

The 500-Word Gap

Have you ever found your mind wandering when listening to someone... be it a conversation or a speech?

One of the serendipitous discoveries along my speaking journey is why that occurs. And it's a vital piece of information for every speaker.

Ralph G Nichols, a long-time Professor of Rhetoric at the University of Minnesota, devoted many of his 96 years to understanding listening. He discovered that the average American speaks about 125 words per minute. He also found that our minds process thoughts as fast as 600-800 words per minute.

He states that our minds continue thinking at a high speed while incoming spoken words are processed at a low speed. Professor Nichols' point? "We can listen and still have spare time for thinking. The use, or misuse, of this spare thinking time holds the answer to how well a person can concentrate on the spoken word."

The excellent book, *Speaker, Leader, Champion* [B3], shows that the speaking rates of eleven recent Toastmasters World Champions of Public Speaking® was an average of 128 words per minute. Now, let's be conservative and choose for their eleven audiences a thought-processing speed at the bottom of Nichol's range of, say, of 628 words per minute. We can therefore assume there is an approximate gap of 500 words per minute (628 minus 128) between what an audience thinks and hears.

This word gap is the biggest challenge every speaker faces—having your audience not just listening attentively to your actual words but having them so engaged and absorbed that you are also capturing the attention of that other 500 words per minute in their minds.

The best way to do this is by developing a strong audience connection using tools highlighted in this toolbox.

Connection Trumps Perfection is the mantra of many speakers. It means that if you are engaging and connecting with your audience, they will be so absorbed, in word and mind, they will overlook Ums and Ahs and other speaking blemishes and much less likely have a wandering mind.

Focus on capturing and engaging your audience.

Intent

The quotations from all sources used in this book have been chosen to illustrate excellence.

In adherence to the "fair use" rule of the U.S. copyright law, this book makes limited use of copyrighted excerpts from the Toastmasters World Championship of Public Speaking® for the purpose of criticism and commentary, and for the purpose of providing a public good by elevating presentation skills of aspiring speakers. As indicated by my association with Toastmasters going back over 50 years, it is my hope that this book significantly increases the number of people exposed to the organization and its mission.

THE SPEAKER'S TOOLBOX

Address the Basics

The three basics of a successful speech are:

1. **Message:** A clear message
2. **Connection:** A speaker-audience connection
3. **Retention:** Your message is remembered (retained)

The image on the opposite page captures these three basics. If you want your speech to soar and score, the message must be Clear, and kicked high between the uprights of Connection and Retention.

Connection is critical because listeners' minds wander and, if you aren't connecting, they keep wandering. Retention is critical because if you are delivering a message and the audience doesn't remember it, your speech is wasted. Simply expressed, *If they can't repeat it, they didn't get it.*[PF]

One way to prepare your speech is to write out your message or key point and keep refining it as you prepare until it is 12 words or less. Then you will clearly know what your speech is about—and so will your audience. Then, as you connect, hold their attention and plant hooks in your speech so that they will readily remember its message.

As you write and review your speech drafts you will think of appropriate Connection and Retention tools from this toolbox to help you deliver a successful speech. Below are some suggested initroductory tools. You will discover others to add to each column to help you build even better speeches as you delve further into your toolbox.

Message + Connection + Retention = Score (Big!)

Connection
Connecting Conversationally
Connecting via Asides
Connecting via Participation
Connecting via Questions
Speech Opening
Twists

Retention (Remembering)
Memory Hooks
Metaphors
Phrase That Stays
Repetition
Speech Closing
Vive la Différence

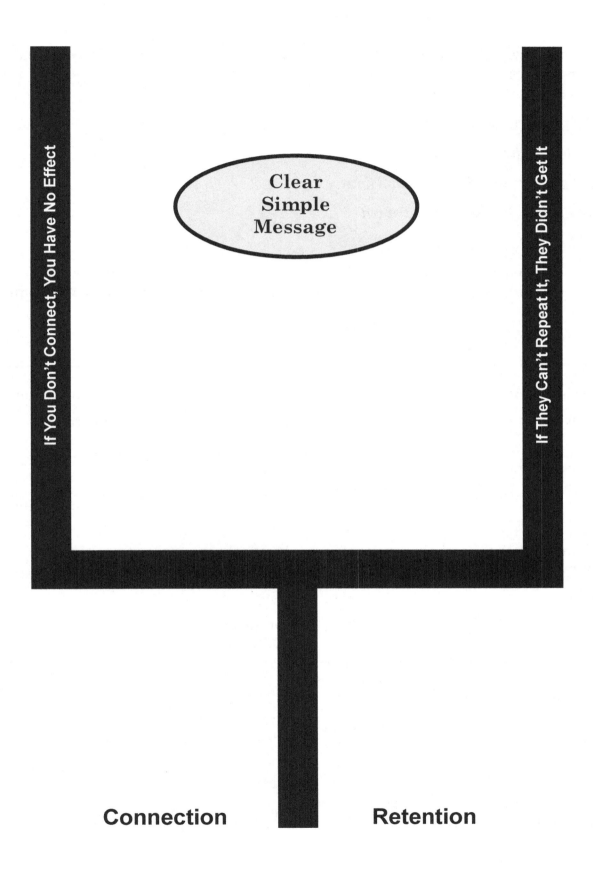

Alliteration

An introductory definition of **Alliteration** is when two or more nearby words have the same first letter or letter sound (eg, f and ph). The words need not necessarily rhyme. Examples are:

It helps when you have a meaningful, memorable message.

Phil had a diabolical dedication to deadlines.

Fred photographed five famous figures

She skedaddled like a scalded cat

Did he kill for the code?

Alliteration appeals because it catches our ear, enriches a speech's rhythm, and enables easier recall. Because it connects and highlights important words, alliteration is frequently found in speech titles and headlines.

Allow the following to activate your alliteration antennae:

A sailor is seasoned in stormy seas.

And he went on to make it contemptuously clear...[79-3]

And when at some future date the high court of history sits in judgment on each one of us...[JFK]

Are we looking for the huge, high drops of disappointment or the twisting turns of ill-fated failure? [04-3]

Five score years ago, a great American, in whose symbolic shadow we stand today, signed the Emancipation Proclamation. [MLK]

Four score and seven years ago our fathers brought forth on this continent a new nation...[AL]

He brings hope to the helpless, calm to the chaos. [15MA]

He fiddles, frets, fritters and flits.

He had at his disposal the coinage of corruption—money and jobs.

He has the shape and substance of fog.

He was too mild to be memorable...

I was into hope and happiness. [15-JJ]

Is American primacy past its peak?

It was a sticky, steamy Indian Summer day.[11AT]

It was the whimper of a wimp.

Latté Liberals and Chardonnay Conservatives

Literature is literally littered with lively legends. [09]

Living intentionally means mustering the mundane moments of life. [15GA]

Many fear the future. Many seek only to satisfy their private work. [BJ]

Mario Andretti she wasn't. More like Molasses Mindy! [DW]

Not a single star of hope hovers over his horizon. [CS]

Our club's culture is our secret sauce.

Our everyday discussions were often no more than a replaying of a litany of canned conversation pieces.

Prepare, pursue, perform, and you will prevail. ᴷᴹ

Success is not final, failure is not fatal: it is the courage to continue that counts. ᵂᶜ

That blow from Shelly sent me spiraling into a deep, dark dungeon of despair. ¹⁰ᴿᴰ

The canvas is no place for a champion. ¹⁰⁻ᴵᴴ

The future is a foreign country—they do things differently there. ᴬᶜᶜ

The sky painter painted vibrant colors with such passion and power that the colors absorbed particles of his own power into the colors he melded. ᴬᴮ·

The smart and the skilled get paid vastly more than the dumb and the dropouts, regardless of whether they come from Birmingham or Bangalore. ᴺᶠ

This will take a month of Mondays.

Toil is the father of fame. ᴱ

The Terrible Twos—that point in a child's development where that precious little toddler turns into a diabolical demon of destruction. ⁹⁷⁻ᶠᴹ

Transit satellites are helping our ships at sea to steer a safer course. ᴶᶠᴷ

Truman's campaign cash cupboard was bare. Corporate chieftains came calling, carrying cashiers' checks. ᴮᵂ·

Use the power of the pause. ᴬᴮ·

We are molded by our parents and our peers, our education and environment; we are products both of nature and of nurture. ⁹⁵⁻³

We are prisoners of our past.

We endured rather than enjoyed the event.

Whisper words of wisdom, let it be. ᵀᴮ

Alliteration in Threes

America is a kaleidoscope of cultures, customs and complexions.

Both football and politics are costly extravaganzas that feed the nation's appetite for competition, consumerism, and carnivalesque stunts. ᴶᵂ⁺

Depressed, disgusted and downtrodden, I contemplated my future. ⁰⁴⁻³

From carefree to care-worn to careless.

Government is big, bloated, and broken.

It's a situation that will end in chaos, conflict, and crisis.

Let's not strangle new ideas in a web of indifference, ignorance, and inaction.

Patience, perseverance, and persistence were their trademarks.

The All Blacks showed the world how rugby should be played—with pride, passion, and panache. ᴸᴺ

The problem was my unwillingness to bend more—to adjust, to adapt, to accept—to pull less. ¹⁵⁻³

They represent colleagues, competitors, customers. ᴷᴬ

Whatever you aspire to be—chemist, carpenter, or clown. ¹⁴⁻ˢᴰ

Your speech was marvelous, meaningful and majestic. ᴹᵀ·

Amplification

Amplification is expanding a statement with one or more explanatory particulars. The particulars usually include descriptive lists and additional words that take you from the base statement to a broader, richer, or more colorful understanding of that statement.

Amplification can be readily seen in these two simple sentences:

Truman had read the Bible—Genesis to Revelation—before he'd started school.

Not six days, not six months, but six years she waited for her husband's return.

Amplification is like adding colors to enrich a scene being painted.

In the 1960 Rome Olympics
She ran for the whole world.
To the French—
She was known as La Gazelle.
To the Italians—the Black Pearl.
And to the rest of the world—
Her friends—and especially her 18
brothers and sisters
She was known as Wilma Rudolph—
The fastest woman in the world. [87]

I was on a new Kawasaki,
A big Bike!
I hit a swarm of bugs.
There were thousands of them
Well—hundreds of them
OK—there was only one!
But it was a BIG one... [DW.]

After all, I'm only a generation-and-a-half from "The Greatest Generation." This makes me 28 percent great, the rest being a combination of neuroses, beer, movies quotes, golf lies, stories that used to be cute but are now offensive, more beer, a clicking sound in my left knee, and a tendency to digress. [CM]

AIDS is not a political creature. It does not care whether you are Democrat or Republican; it does not ask whether you are black or white, male or female, gay or straight, young or old. [MF]

All of us have times when we get punched, get tilted, or completely knocked to the ground. And strangely, it doesn't matter if you are rich or poor, black, white, yellow or red, and it doesn't matter if you live in the inner city or a rural community. [06]

And you wonder why you have your ups and downs and goods and bads and backs and forths and bottoms and tops and ins and outs—the bottom line is that you've turned your back on your spirit. [99]

Another style is the Blues—deals with the hardship and sadness of life, with subjects like the dog died, the man cheated, the heart is broken, lost my job, can't pay the rent, woman left me, took the kids AND the pink Cadillac with the diamond in the back. [02]

At 35 I met an amazing woman, a beautiful woman, smart woman—a woman embraced by an aura of yes. [10-2]

At Westminster College, in Fulton, Missouri, on March 5, 1946, Churchill declared a stark reality: "From Stettin in the Baltic to Trieste in the Adriatic, an iron curtain has descended across the Continent" [Note: the seas amplify the cities]

Grammie turned 100—yeah! It's triple digits. It's twenty-five leap years; it's like reaching 100,000 miles on the odometer of life. She's even 10 years older than Toastmasters! [15EF]

I faced this problem: Do I want to fit in, or do I want to stand up, stand out and stand fast for who and what I am; do I want to be same or different? [09]

I sat across from a troubled student. I looked into his eyes—dark eyes, empty eyes. [04RH]

I walked into cousin Will's room. There were trophies, cups, and ribbons everywhere—swimming, archery, football, horseback riding. [09-3]

If, when you say whiskey, you mean the devil's brew, the poison scourge, the bloody monster, that defiles innocence, dethrones reason, destroys the home, creates misery... [NS]

It's not a trickle of emotion. It's a roaring flood, a tidal wave of feeling that lifts you up and carries you along for a ride. [JM]

Me? Getting older? Oh, No—No —No!!! I am not ready for Bingo, and shuffleboard, and Jeopardy, and Wheel of Fortune, and Florida, and cruises—and Cracker Barrel. [16SJ]

Now, this lanky cosmetically challenged gentleman is the kind of person that most of you would call a born loser. At the age of 31 he failed in business; at 34 he failed in business again; at 43, 46, and 48 he ran for a position as senator—each time he was defeated, but at the age of 56 he ran for the Vice Presidency and guess what happened? Guess what happened? He failed again. Given this turn of events he has this delusion that one day he will be the President [laughs]—he made it! At the age of 60 Abraham Lincoln was elected President. [02-3]

Of course, at 29, I'm doing the usual things people do when they have a mid-life crisis: swearing off of sun tanning, investing in anti-aging creams, considering Botox, performing a salsa dance routine in a sparkly costume, running half-marathons, doing the Master Cleanser 8-day liquid fast, joining Match.com, reliving all of my failed relationships, quitting my job and moving to South America and—entering humorous speech contests. [RR.]

One of my favorite cereals is Choco Crunch, featuring a character named Chockle the Blob—a name that took six minutes and an equal number of beers to come up with ... [CM]

That receptionist had just made my day. Heck, she made my month! With one little "Chi-chink" [05]

The team was needing a Hail Mary, a rabbit's foot, a four-leaf clover and a presidentil pardon. [MR^]

Two years ago our son woke up at the crack of "Jeopardy!", packed the essentials—15 pairs of gym shorts, five pairs of shoes of varying sizes, 22 boxes of Pop-Tarts, and every video game ever made and headed off for college. [CM]

We can start our own business. We can start a factory. We can even sell fake American goods—to Americans! [11-2]

Within a 5-week period, I lost my job, my apartment, and my girlfriend. If I had lost a dog and an old pickup truck, I would have had a country music song. [12-ML]

You can set any destination you want [on my GPS]. Even choosing the shortest or the fastest route. Or, if you have kids, the fast food route through McDonald's. [10-3]

Connecting Conversationally

Today, a speech is a conversation—a dialogue, not a monologue. A speaker does not talk *to* an audience–he talks *with* them.

Good conversations involve interaction, primarily mental engagement. For example, the simple question, "Have you ever been talking to someone when…?" has your listeners answering the question in their minds while simultaneously awaiting what you will say next.

Likewise, as in a conversation, listeners like to be acknowledged and included. When someone speaks mostly about himself, listeners' attention begins to wander.

"You's" tell your listeners they are important. To connect and get your message across, professional speakers stress having a high You/I ratio, ie, having many more "You's" than "I's." Having four "You's" in the speech for each "I" in a speech is a good objective.

Speeches with more "You's and We's" than "I's and Me's" are more effective at gaining attention. The following shows different ways speakers have accomplished this:

"You" is preferable to "I"

[Takes red rose from his vest pocket and smells it] You and I are not very different from this flower. Just like this flower is unique, you are unique…Do you know what makes you special? [14]
[Speech opening]

Do you realize how much green fees and golf cart fees contribute to the gross national product? Billions! [83]

Don't you hate it when parents are right? [12]

Every relationship started with great expectations and ended in great depression. Have you had problems in your relationships? How did you fix it? [15-3]

Have you ever been judged before somebody got to know you? How did it make you feel? [RD]

I had some of those things. You probably have some of them, too!—Don't tell me you don't! [97]

I looked at my reflection and asked him the same question you are probably asking me right now—"What?" And he slowed it down for me, and I'd like to do that for you today. He said… [99]

I was the kind of kid your parents told you not to play with. You probably remember me—the Detention Hall's only permanent resident! [98]

I went back home that night, and as you can imagine, all I wanted was to be alone. [15-2]

I went to the one woman I trust—my mama …"Mama, I want a wife." She said, "No problem. We can fix it." Ladies and gentlemen, did you hear what my mama said? [15-3]

I'll bet that you're all like Mark Twain, who said: *I've received many compliments in my life—was embarrassed by all of them—they were all far too short!!* [03-BW]

If you want to have, do or be something better, you've got to start by doing something different. [15-JJ]

8

Listen, it's in your hearts right now. [91]

Many of you are wondering the same thing I was. What's sickle cell? [10]

Maybe you know what it's like to sit at the bedside of someone who's dying. [15PH]

No matter what zip code you live in...

Maybe you wanted to...

Right now, you are probably thinking...

Statistically, you shouldn't be here today. Your ancestors faced countless obstacles. War. Disease. The British Empire. Yet against all the odds, and this early start, you made it here today. You are truly a miracle. [12-03]

Well, you know the answer to that... [91]

You and I know [FDR] [A favorite phrase in FDR's radio messages]

You already know this, but...

You know what she said... [94-2]

You should have seen the look on Jackie's face when I asked her, "Do you remember how we first met?" [10]

You're all impressed—I can tell [01]

Your own books belong to you; you treat them with that affectionate intimacy that annihilates formality ... you should own no book that you are afraid to mark up [WLP]

"We" (and "Us") is preferable to "Me"

All of us have something special that makes us as beautiful. [14]

And he reminded us of what we've all known since we were children: to make a difference, all we need are three silver bullets: honor, integrity and self-respect. Yes, in more ways than one, we can come home again. [90]

Here's the choice we face...

I—like many of us here—have dreamed impossible dreams. [09]

Ours is a throwaway society and we do it with people as well as machines. Unfortunately, sometimes we do it to ourselves when we quit work prematurely. [83]

Somewhere along the way we learned a painful truth. We learned that failing to achieve our dream hurts. We encounter critics, who ridicule and crush our dream, and it hurts. We hear an inner voice that cries out, "No more." [03]

This we must do for our children. [FDR]

We are a people in a quandary about the present. We are a people in search of our future. We are a people in search of a national community. We are a people trying not only to solve the problems of the present ... but we are attempting on a larger scale to fulfill the promise of America. [BJ]

We are surrounded by...

We've seen this before, haven't we?

Whether we like it or not—everything in life is arranged. [VJ]

Why, in just the past three years we've seen an Olympic athlete stripped of his gold medals because he used drugs. We've seen not one, but two television ministers fall from grace. We've seen billionaires bankrupted by greed. And we've seen Donald Trump...be Donald Trump. [90]

Yes, we all hunger for recognition, don't we? And we all love to receive it. [03-BW]

You can change a life, inspire a nation, make this world a beautiful place. Isn't that what we all want? Isn't that why we are all in this hall? [15]

Connecting via Asides

Sometimes when giving a speech, adding an offhand comment, explanation, or amusing point allows you to verbally check in with your audience, clarify what you are saying, provide a little bit of "inside information," change the direction, relax the tempo, or simply evoke a smile. Such additions are referred to in speaking as **Asides**.

They can be as simple as:

Now, just between you and me...

You can't make this stuff up...

Oh, I almost forgot...

They draw your listeners a little closer to you. As speeches are dialogues, speech Asides maintain your connection and allow your listeners keep pace with your thought process.

Some speakers have taken Asides almost to an art form. The first three examples that follow are taken from just one engaging speech. The others examples demonstrate the diversity of this excellent connection tool.

I was about to tell Joanna my plans when the Universe changed them: My blood sugar dropped dramatically. When your brain springs into corrective action, you lose emotional control and rational thought—You know, those are a couple of things you don't need on a first date! [01-LL]

Next month I turn 50. Only this morning I was thinking there is no way I can really be that old—as I took my blood pressure medicine! [01-LL]

She notices I'm starting to look a little goofy. Okay—goofier than usual. [01-LL]

As I took note of the perfectly rounded weight I could only say "Wow!—Now, backwards, that's WOW! [06]

At 8, I finally rode my bike. To celebrate, my mother and I took the training wheels off—Don't get excited, we only took them off the front wheel! [96]

Baby, you can get on that stage and say that speech, or you can get on that stage and look like a fool—You noticed there was a part that wasn't optional. [08]

CRACK!! (Tree limb breaks). A-h-h-h (Slowly begins to fall)—Have you ever noticed that life-changing events always seem to happen in slow motion? [06-2]

Even today, we are judged by the color of our hair—well, some of us! [RD.]
[The speaker was bald]

He's a crazy nut case—that's a technical term. [TC^]

I asked her, "How long have you been in the game?"—Translation: "How long have you been prostituting?" [15-PH]

I became a wannabe entrepreneur. This man offered me buckets of money to build him a website. New car, here I come! [12]

I broke the first rule of changing a tire—choose a level spot! Friends, in Chicago there aren't that many slopes, but that night I found one—Why do flat tires always happen when you are dressed up? [Taking jacket off and putting on floor] [13]

I did it my way (singing)—I never said I was singing well. [99]

I kept my good looks—well, most of them—well, that's what my mother said. [10-3] [Double Aside]

I rejoined Toastmasters—despite its strange rituals. [10-3]

I settled in this country, found an engineering job, became a father and got married — Not exactly in that order. [JA10]

I turned to my two sons, and said: "Guys, what did you learn from this?" My16-year old said…" I learned that my dad cries at the movies." My 12-year old took the question—and his wellbeing—a bit more seriously. [03]

I was a teenager and my parents were desperate—sounds familiar doesn't it? [07]

I'm five foot four—when I'm really trying. [08]

I've 4 principles—aptly named 1 to 4. [80]

Incomes are falling—as I'm sure you've noticed—

It's dark. I'm in a barn with no electric power. There's a cow strapped to a post with a rope. And back here is a cold cowboy aiming his flashlight, poorly—Would you like to talk about a bad day at the office? [94]

Let me tell the Democrats, let me tell the mainstream media—although I repeat myself. [TC^]

Many, many times, I would don the armor of righteousness; mount my trusty grey horse; Yeeeha!—Work with me here!—[09]

Mother had a bright idea—Oh, this one was a gem! [97]

My 9-year old brother was poised on the 12-foot high diving board. He didn't swim. Hadn't seen water except for a bathtub—and we couldn't get him in that. [97-2]

My motorcycle hit the trees … they were slapping my face—At least they cleaned the bugs off my goggles! [DW.]

Heaven knows that I cannot wait
To get off this stage and get some clothes back on—
And that's a sentence I never thought I'd have to say. [16KH]

One evening I hear this huge crash—
And then—something worse—silence!
I come careening down the stairs
To see my youngest son lying on the floor
Amongst a slew of decapitated Greek gods.
Funny sentence—not a funny scene. [16-KH]

The car was swerving this way and that—it's a good thing I missed the bridge abutment. [04RH]

Then I got hooked [on meditation]—Did you know meditation was cool? [07]

There are millions of people out there who can't afford a single pair of shoes. Many of us have 20 pairs—ladies 50 pairs. [12-2]

There you go Mr Tate. Next time, drive a little slower. Speaking of slow—have you ever wondered why it takes a police officer so long to write a ticket? [00]

They won't discriminate against you because of your grey hair—or lack of it—you grey panthers and bald eagles. [83]

Twice I took 6 months off to travel the world—of course, that was before I was married.

Connecting via Participation

Historically, speeches have been formal oratory—a one-way communication or monologue. In contrast, today's highly connected world of media outlets asking what we think, internet polls, Facebook "Likes," and other opinion-centered interactions illustrate that people desire a participative dialogue.

How can you involve your audience? One of the easiest ways is to simply ask your audience to imagine something (relative to your speech). Another approach is inviting your audience to participate by doing, saying, or shouting out something.

Tom Hopkins, a professional speaker, states: "If I say it, they can doubt me. But if they say it, it is true to them. So get the audience to repeat or say out loud the ideas you want internalized." For this reason, *engaging*, as opposed to *telling*, your audience increases the chance they will remember both you and your message.

The following examples present ideas as to how you might experiment with inviting your audience to participate in your speeches:

Imagine

Imagine if you were born into a home with no books...[5 second pause] [RW.]
[This was the grabber opening to a memorable speech on tackling illiteracy.]

Imagine a world without computers, the Internet, or your cell phone—which would you miss most? Why?...

Imagine my parents' reaction—"I want to be a comedian!" [01]

Invitation to Join the Speaker

Come back with me to 1948—Harry Truman's campaign cupboard is bare... [An invitation to see the scene with you, not just hear you talk of it.]

Come with me to Ancient Greece. One sculptor, Pygmalion, loved his statue so much it turned into life. [86]

Join me on a journey into Space. [BW.]

Let's do something together. [15JO]

May I invite you to visit my Swimming Club? [Arm out, moving to Stage Left]

Invitation to Participate

A multi-invitation to participate was given by Rich Hopkins. Rich invited the audience to Let's play Complete the Cliché: *If only we knew then*—[Audience response] *What we know now.* What if we reverse the scene? *What if we knew now what we knew*—[Audience response] *then.* With participation established, Rich later ended his speech with these lines: *Come on, get up! Stand up with me! Hands in the air! Shout with me: Good Morning!!!!*—His audience responded by helping Rich close his speech, standing and shouting with their hands in the air—and enjoying it! [06-3]

Hands up those who have or have had teenagers...[pause, looks around]...Ah, the Fellowship of Suffering! [JK]

How many of you have been hurt by another person? Put your hands up. I know you have. I want you to repeat after me: I've been bitten...
[Audience] *I've been bitten...*
But it didn't kill me...
[Audience] *But it didn't kill me.* [CV]

How many of you have children? [Wait for response.] How many of you are still children? [Wait for laughter.]

How many of you remember a teacher who made a difference in your life? On the count of three, shout out loud his or her name. RH

In the *speech The Ultimate Question* the audience was asked: Do you validate (ie, appreciate or recognize) others? We then "see" a receptionist validating a parking ticket with her machine sounding off *cha-ching*. Over 20 more *cha-chings* later (validating others), the speech ends with audience participation as they answer three times the speaker's repeated question: Can you *cha*-[audience response: *ching*]? Can you cha-[*ching*]? Can you cha-[*ching*]? 05

Join me in singing the Barney song. 01-2

Let's close with some fun! I want you to sit up in your chairs and when I signal I want you to shout *Rematch!*

If you miss out on that job promotion you desperately want, what will you say? [Audience] *Rematch!*

If you lock yourself out of your house in your underwear, what will you say? [Audience] *Rematch!*

If I get rejected on another date, what will I say?
[Audience] *Rematch!* 10LC

Let's practice that together: *I'm proud of you!* Now let's say it so others can hear it: [Audience] *I'm proud of you!!*
One more time, shout it so your kids at home can hear it:
[Audience] *I'm proud of you!!!* 93-RS

Our three inmates, Mother Teresa, Abraham Lincoln, and Nelson Mandela are in here because they did the incredible. They dedicated their whole lives to their ideals. They pursued their goals with unparalleled resilience. They did, in other words, what we all agreed is—[waits for audience reply] *crazy*. I can't hear you—it's [everyone says] *crazy*. 02-3
[The speech was titled *Crazy*.]

Sitting next to you … may be the friend of your heart, or of your times, or of your blood—Reach out now in your mind—and heart—and touch them.[11]

So all of you take off your shoes right now! [Speaker had become shoeless early in the speech.] I don't want to be alone. Come on—take them off. I'm serious! Take your shoes off and look at them— tell yourself—no one can fit into these shoes better than me.[12-2]

The best role model of all was—wait— let's see if you remember. I'm going to start a famous phrase and I want you to finish it when I give you this cue (hand moves as if twirling a lasso). But remember, we do things BIG down here, so I want them to hear you from Singapore to San Antonio. Are you ready? Then return with me to those thrilling days of yesteryear… *A fiery horse with the speed of light, a cloud of dust and a hearty* [Audience response: *Hi-Yo Silver! Away!*] Yes! The Lone Ranger rides again— Makes you feel good, doesn't it? 90

Without these two tiny words, our world would not exist. Do you want to know what they are? Say yes.
[Audience responds: *Yes!*][12-3]

Connecting via Questions

Asking your audience a question increases their interest. It creates a feeling of inclusion—even when the question simply requires thought, with no verbal response or action. When the word "you" is included in the question, it tells each listener that you are talking directly to him or her.

Questions are very effective in building a bond with your audience. An example of such a speech was WCPS Darren LaCroix's *Ouch!*[01] Engagement was strengthened by questions in the opening, closing, and at nine points in between! This is a strong rate—about 1.5 questions per minute.

LaCroix's questions were not only seamlessly woven into his speech but were strongly and directly supportive of his message. To illustrate:

- *Can you remember a moment when a brilliant idea flashed into your head?*
- *What do you do when you fall on your face? Do you try to jump right up and hope no one noticed?*
- *Do you feel I stayed down to long? Have YOU ever stayed down too long?*
- *What changes would you like to make in your life? What is your next step?*

Other examples of speakers connecting via questions follow:

Can you imagine the shock on my face when they announced that [my mother] this rock, this powerhouse, this Shaq in a wig—that her cancer was beyond treatment? And do you know what she said? [08]

Can you picture how colorful the bank was that morning? [99-2]
[Speaker describing over 30 Ghanaians in their national formal wear opening a group bank account]

Do you ever feel as if someone else is writing your script—the script of your life? [03-2]

Do you have those people?
Are there those people in your life
Who had such an impact on you
That changed the course of your life
And they might not even remember?
Do you think there are people out there
Whose lives you've changed,
And you don't remember them? [16SS]

Do you know what's bizarre? The winning team was knocked out but they negotiated their way back in. [10LC]

Do you think that anybody cared when Albert Einstein's hair started to turn white? Did physicists stop listening to Stephen Hawking when his entire body revolted against him? If your spark shines brightly enough—people will not care what it's wearing. [16SJ]

Even a teacher said that if I took poetry as a profession, I would most likely starve. Wouldn't those discouraging words deflate your spirit? I felt dejected, and turned away from my passion. [AJ10]

Have you ever been hurt in the game of love? I mean, really hurt.

Have you ever had to tell your dad you'd crashed his car? [LM]

Have you ever looked at modern art and wondered which side is up? [07]

14

Have you ever rehearsed a speech in your car and [turns and waves] stopped because someone is staring at you at a red light? [01-3]

Have you ever wondered why nobody cares about global warming—even though it is a very serious issue? It could kill all of us. [15]

How many of you have mamas like that? How many of you *are* mamas like that? [02-CW]

I found a great girl, but not a job. I didn't know what I wanted to do with my life—Have you ever had that problem? [14]

I kept track of my fears and successes. Was it easy? [Vigorously shakes his head "No."] [01-3]

I parked on a slope leading to a busy street. [I had a flat tire.] Mr. Contest Chair, Toastmasters and Guests—have you even done something stupid? [13]

I reached for the instrument bucket. Forgot my hand was wet. Now here's the science quiz: True or false?—Wet skin freezes fast to super cold metal? [94]

I read the top 20 books on relationships. Guess what? They don't work. [15-3]

If I were to ask you where is the richest place on earth, where would you say it is? Would you say the Toronto Stock Exchange? The Arabic oil wells? Or perhaps the diamond mines in Africa? I submit to you that the richest place on earth is the graveyard. [93]

Let me ask a question that may seem strange today. How many of you know the number of people who have died from snakebite? Answer please? [Audience calls out answers] [CV]

Let me ask you a question that may sound a little strange. How many of you chose your parents? [VJ]

Now, how many of you are husbands in here? Raise your hands. Yeah. I wasn't being unkind when I looked at my wife and said: "You know, those blue jeans look like they don't fit like they used to." Wow! Pain! Agony! Sleeping on the couch. [RH]

Think back. Do you remember the pain you felt when you faced intolerance just because you were different? Do you remember when you faced indifference?—Do you remember how deeply it hurt? [95]

We all have our heroes, don't we?

What makes us different from all other life? Creativity. Everything you do is a result of creativity. This century will be the creative century. [12-3]

When was the last time you saw the extraordinary in the ordinary? [06-3]

Why do I share my story with you? [15-PH]

Checking In

Don't you agree?

What would you do?

Are you still with me?

Does that make sense?

Did I say the day was hot?

Did I say he was a big guy?

Have you ever felt that way?

General Questions

Can you imagine?

Are you ready for this?

Can you remember when..?

Can you guess what this is?

Do you know what happened next?

Ever had one of those days that just crumble before your eyes? [DL]

Hands up if you have heard me before or who is hearing me for the first time? [ZZ]

Connecting via Segments

Another path to connection with your listeners is by engaging different segments of your audience. This is done in various ways including:

- Acknowledging the Chair and audience
- Using the organization's lingo
- Highlighting individuals in the audience
- Pointing out specific groups in the audience

Even though you are addressing only a segment of the audience, everyone usually understands and appreciates it. They feel the added bonding thread it creates. The following shows how different speakers have successfully connected in this way:

Targeted Opening

[To allow for self-selection or aimed at a specific segment.]

[After Speaker explains that he has just parked on a slope with a flat tire]—
Mr. Contest Chair, Toastmasters, and Guests—Have you even done something stupid? [13] [Greeting invites self-selection]

It was a day I'll never forget. I had a date with destiny. On this day I discovered the difference one man can make. Madam Toastmaster, Fellow Toastmasters, and anyone who has had a date with destiny! [AD^] [A fun inclusion to open this humorous speech]

Mr Toastmaster, Fellow Toastmasters, Guests and most vigilant Judges... [12-KRM] [Recognizing rarely-mentioned judges]

Mr. Chairman, fellow Toastmasters, and anyone else who believes that their life is going to come to an end without their smart phone. [14-3]
[*Good-Bye Wi-Fi* was the title. It invites self-selection.]

Mr. Contest Chair, friends—<u>and the people way in the back!</u> [01]
[Spoken lying face down on the stage to a very large audience.]

My mind rewinds like an old school VHS tape. It takes me back to high school when I would plead with my mom to let me go to parties. "Mom, please let me go! There'll be no alcohol—I promise." Mom in her nightgown and bunny slippers smiled sweetly. "All right, I trust you." Mister Contest Chair, Fellow Toastmasters, and anybody who has ever lied to Mama before ... [12] [Title: *Trust is a Must*. Greeting invites self-selection.]

Using Lingo of Organization, Company, or Event

And here we have the friends of my heart ... of lovers. And for me that's my wife Robyn. And I'm lucky there too, because I married a Toastmaster ... and that's Better Thinking. [11] (Laughter)
[*Better Listening, Thinking, Speaking* is Toastmasters founding motto.]

And tell yourself that these shoes are designed for me. Tell yourself that no matter what my role is—at home—at work—or in Toastmasters—no one can fit into these shoes better than me. [12-2] [Reminds audience of their common bond in Toastmasters.]

I told him I did something stupid. I asked for his help. Jesse looked at the car and said, "You were right—that's stupid. Let me show you." [Sound of squeaky jack going up quickly]. I found a DJM—Distinguished Jack Master [laughter]. [13]

If you need a title—be imaginative. If you need a degree, that's simple for you Toastmasters. All you have to do is complete our basic Competent Toastmaster Manual and put CTM behind your name. For all anyone knows CTM means "Master of Computer Technology"—and that's pretty important these days. [83]

No matter how much of an effort I invested in my work, my boss would nit-pick on my performance, even my pronunciation and enunciation. I suspect he was a Toastmaster![16DT]

So my dad introduced me to this strange club that had a strange name with strange people . . . talking. On the first meeting they told me to do something called a Table Topic. I aced it, but while I was speaking ... [14]

When I'm feeling low, I start giving thanks for everything. I'm thankful for the lessons of my marriage the last 24 years; I'm thankful for our son; I'm thankful for Toastmasters; I'm thankful for the chance to be here. I'm thankful that I can breathe and walk and speak and hear. [15-JJ]

Links to Individuals

Col. Travis led 189 men in defending the Alamo against untold thousands of troops led by Gen. Santa Ana. Let's put that in perspective—that's like me and Mr Corcoran against all of you—and I don't even know if he can fight! [02-2]
[Ted Corcoran was the Contest's well-known and popular Contest Chair]

How many new Facebook friends would roll out of bed at 3AM and come to my aid if I needed them? Probably not one! So who can I count on? John Lau says on his Facebook page, "Everyone has a best friend during each stage of life—only a lucky few have the same one." [11]
[John Lau was another well-known and popular Contest Chair.]

I know you're not one. You don't look like one. I'm certain you're not one. [Each time pointing to individual members of audience.] And I'm not one either—Or are we? Mr Toastmaster and Friends, perhaps we are all thieves? ... [03BW]
[Each audience member singled out feels special; others wonder if they will be called out next.]

Links to Segments

Whenever I get frustrated or angry with the people around me—and next time you get frustrated or angry with the people around you—maybe they've shopped too many times at KLCC [local Dept Store]—Maybe they got up late and that's why you're sitting up there [points up to the balcony]. Give them the positive four words because at the end of the day, everything's gonna be—"okay." [14-2]
[An original way to connect with those in the balcony]

There was one person I was very afraid of—my mama. Raise your hand if you have an emotional mother. Put them all together and you'll get my "Mama." I could hear her scream. Even the cops were afraid! ... [later] ... Now my dad is a cool dad. Raise your hand if you have a cool dad. Put them all together and you get my dad.
[Cleverly includes everyone ... both women and men!] [14]

Contrast

Contrast is following a word, phrase or idea with an opposite one, which usually acts as a balance. Contrasts appeal because there is unity and memorability in opposites, such as love and hate, remember and forget, win or lose. Its balancing, attention-getting effect freshens and gives life to your speech. It also highlights the point you wish to make.

One of Contrast's best-known examples is the opening of Dickens' *A Tale of Two Cities*, the biggest selling novel in history:

It was the best of times, it was the worst of times,
it was the age of wisdom, it was the age of foolishness,
it was the season of Light, it was the season of Darkness,
it was the spring of hope, it was the winter of despair ...

Use the following examples to help concoct your own creative Contrasts:

A lie gets halfway around the world before the truth has a chance to get its pants on. [WC]

At four, great is a brand-new Barbie, grief is a brand-new brother. [09-CN]

Before the accident [which put me in this wheelchair], I saw the world from an invincible 6 feet high—now I see it from the height of the consummate navel gazer. [09]

By "retirement" I mean the sudden stoppage of work, going from the dynamic career to the doldrums, from vigor to vegetation. [83]

Clem Pinckney always had the biggest presence in the room; he also had the smallest ego. [RT]

Destiny is not a matter of chance; it's a matter of choice. [WJB]

English majors may not be the first hired—but they are the first promoted. [KC]

Equal rights for all, special privileges for none. [TJ]

Every relationship started with great expectations and ended in great depression. [15-3]

Grandma, now there's a word filled with memories: most of them good—the rest of them good for you. [07-RK]

He didn't answer me. Or did he? [99]

He had no place to go and all the time in the world to go there. [LC]

His people are many: they are like the grass that covers vast prairies. My people are few: they resemble the scattering trees of a storm-swept plain. [CS]

I bear a message of challenge, not self-congratulation; I want your attention, not your applause. [MF]

I grew up in Pakistan; Linda grew up in Texas. I was mocha; she was latte. I was a PC; she was a Macintosh. What a love fest! [SN]

I had changed everything in my life, but nothing had changed. [05]

I have fought against white domination and I have fought against black domination. I have cherished the ideal of a democratic and free society ... an ideal which I hope to live for ... but if needs be, it is an ideal for which I am prepared to die. [NM]

I know what I'm saying; I just don't know what you're hearing. [MA]

I remember the US women's gymnastics team that competed in the 1996 Olympics. They had an athlete, Kerri Strug. Kerri was the one with the heart of a giant and the voice of a Munchkin. [98-RB]

I shouted to my mama: "I'm not doing it." My world stood still—my mama stood up. [08]

I'd rather be disliked for what I am, than liked for what I am not. [MJ.]

If you destroy a free market, you create a black market. [WC]

In a time in which the famous are becoming infamous, when contemptible behavior is becoming commonplace, maybe it's time we looked beyond mere symbols. [90]

In an ordinary kitchen, I learnt an extraordinary lesson. [09]

Many, many times, I would don the armor of righteousness … raise my lance and charge into hell for my heavenly cause. [09]

My message is not about delivery of a new life; it's about deliverance from an old life. [94]

My support system appeared in unexpected places—and disappeared from expected places. [10PH]

Patriotism is not the fear of something; it is the love of something. [AS]

She is beautiful, and I'm just some punk with pimples. [12]

So I turn off their Wi-Fi and they turn on their creative minds. [14-3]

Sometimes in the springtime in life—when young blood courses through vibrant veins; sometimes later in life—when sluggish blood cruises through varicose veins. [11]

Sometimes we're the judge; sometimes we're the jury. [10RD]

The ballot is stronger than the bullet. [AL]

The first half of your life is controlled by your parents; the second half by your kids. [LM]

The further backward we can look, the further forward we can see. [WC]

This Fourth of July is yours, not mine. You may rejoice, I must mourn. [FD]

This is not a distant threat. It is a present danger. [MF]

United, there is little we cannot do— Divided, there is little we can do. [JFK]

We are so fixated on what could be that we lose focus on what it is. [12-2]

We beat fear with hope. We beat cynicism with hard work. We beat negative, divisive politics with a positive vision that brings Canadians together. [JT]

We cannot become what we need to be by remaining what we are. [MP]

We could all tell a thousand stories, each nothing in itself but all adding up to something wonderful. [11]

We have perpetual war for perpetual peace. [GV]

We owed them our loyalty—they owed us sound judgment. [JW]

You can walk hand in hand without seeing eye-to-eye. [RW]

You can't help the face you were born with but you can help the expression you wear on it. Beauty might only be skin deep but ugly goes down forever. [94-3]

Details

Details add depth to a speech. They sharpen the image of characters, events, and scenes that you describe. They bring your audience more fully "into the picture" and, in so doing, add realism and authenticity to your words.

The sharper and clearer the details, the more memorable the scene. Details are noticed; bland is invisible. For example: *He cruised comfortably to a stop in his silver Lexus* paints a sharper, clearer picture than *He stopped his car.*

Details help greatly but it's best to avoid excessive doses. They add a touch of difference in as little as one sentence. For example:

- *I spent weeks glued to a screen, typing on a Cheetos-stained keyboard[12]*

- *When I was sixteen Fat Dad bought me a 63 Volkswagen Beetle: gray, wide tires, chrome wheels, and bucket seats.[04]*

- *It was 5:01 in the afternoon; the town clock had just struck, and the storm clouds were becoming darker, meaner, more threatening …*

A handful of sharp simple details give us a clear picture: it may be a factual description, a statement of pride, or it's setting the mood for what follows, as do the three examples above.

You will see in the examples that follow the roles details play in painting a clearer, more realistic, and more authentic scene for the audience to appreciate and enjoy:

It was March 4th, 1993. I remember this date for a number of reasons. Number one, because it was my last collegiate basketball game ever. Number two, because of my 22nd birthday, and Number three, because of what my ex-girlfriend did that night. Emphasis on ex. (Audience laughter) Changed the course of my life. [CV]

A six-foot-two redhead is America's greatest architect. Thomas Jefferson was the architect of Monticello, the Virginia State Capitol, the University of Virginia, and he drafted the blueprint for our nation—the Declaration of Independence. [BW.]

"Andy, can you please clean that up?" He would say "Yeah, I'll do it later." The Coke cans, chip wrappers, candy wrappers, orange peels—later. [14-2]

As I sat there alone, I realized I was the only one without some sort of device in my hand. There were people in the pool with their cell phones. There were people at the bar with a drink in one hand and a smart phone in the other. No one was admiring the beautiful, blue sea. Instead they were watching movies and reading books on their tablets.[14-3]

At dinnertime, as we sat there on those ugly orange Naugahyde chairs I looked at her through the mystic steam rising off the roast beef, carrots, and potatoes. I asked her … [04RH]

Dad, how did you manage to get through that?" He looked at me: "Son, the lesson I learned is this—Those that judge you, don't deserve you. Even today we are judged by the color of our hair, whether we have tattoos or piercings, the clothes we wear, the cars we drive, where we live, our race, our religion, and yes, the color of our skin. Sometimes we are the judges, and sometimes we are the jury." 10-RD

He had gray thinning hair, tucked behind his ears. His tan khakis were neatly pressed and had a paper-cut-sharp crease, white button-down shirt. Had the sleeves neatly folded up to his elbows. As he turned to walk, I noticed a familiar grimace and a familiar limp. "Knee or hip?" 11AT

I know a remarkable teen-aged girl Nicole, and you should know that she is hearing impaired, vision impaired—and three years ago she survived a stroke. I've watched Nicole redefine reality not according to her physical limitations, but according to the size of her dreams. As part of that, two years ago, I saw her stand on a huge stage before almost three thousand people, and perform the sweetest song I've never heard. She sang it with sign language that I didn't just see, but deep inside, I felt it! 03

I noticed a tall, handsome, young man. He was perfect, with his fresh haircut, black tailored blazer, and pearly white smile. 16DB

I was not funny. I was not a class clown. In fact the first time my brother ever laughed at me was when I told him I was going to be a comedian. 01

I was relaxing on the couch, watching the New York Knicks beat the Orlando Magic, when my very pregnant wife says ... 12ML

In the gas station behind the counter stood a big man with a big smile. Badge read— Jesse. 13

My momma wasn't laughing though. When I got home that night I wasn't laughing either. She treated me to a hickory stick waltz. You know what I mean—a piece of kindling taken from the wood box applied to the backside in steady rhythms. You sing along in keys, chords, and crescendos. 04RH

My brother was not due out [of prison] until 1997. I had learned that people diagnosed with colon cancer at that time—Stage 4 colon cancer, to be specific—only had about a four-to-six month window to live—March, April, May, June, July, August, 1996. My mother is in Daniel Freeman Hospital lying on her deathbed. 15PH

Tears rolled down my cheeks as I remembered the wonderful years I had spent with him when I was a kid. I saw myself playing in his small house in Calcutta, those hot summer days I spent playing in his backyard, his caring hug, his gentle smile. VJ

There's a tiny, tumbleweed town called Leadore, Idaho, that God has designated a winter misery test site. There the bitter wind blows, and it drives the cold to the marrow of your bones. 94

Thinking of our family get-togethers I can still see Grandpapa sitting off to one side of the room [Speaker walks and sits on chair]—A tin of tobacco between his knees rolling another cigarette [Speaker licks it sealed]—Unreachable in his silence as if his shyness chained him to his chair. 01-3

Emotions—Discovering Them

Emotions move the heart; the heart moves audiences.

Emotions are one of the most powerful tools in your toolbox. Almost twenty-five centuries ago, Aristotle wrote they are one of the three pillars of persuasion.

Some speakers naturally show emotion when speaking. Many, including many introverts, do not. Fortunately there are ways to raise your emotional quotient as a speaker. The first is to identify what your current emotional status is: what emotions trigger more readily than others for you and what types of topics trigger them? The second, of course, is to speak on subjects that you care about, topics that activate your emotions. To paraphrase Churchill: Before a speaker can inspire an audience with any emotion he must be swayed himself. Before he can move their tears his own must flow.

There are six primary emotions[DB]—Happiness, Surprise, Sadness, Anger, Disgust, and Fear, each with many gradations. Some years ago I was at a meeting devoted to discovering our emotions. The leader[RS.] gave each attendee the Discover Your Emotions sheet, opposite, and asked us to follow the directions:

1. Write down 6 memories, each incorporating one of the emotions.
2. Select 3 of them and briefly explain what each meant to you.
3. Select 1 of those 3, and explain the message you'd like to share.

It was a fast and simple funnel approach to identifying some big and small events in our past that still carry emotional memories (even for those who usually avoid displaying emotion). As we moved to steps 2 and 3, it became clearer which were more sensitive than others.

Each participant ended the exercise with the core of an emotion-laced speech. Some of the participants even delivered the speech they developed the same night!

If you wish to test your emotional status, or if you are just looking for a speech with an emotional base, complete this sheet. It's an excellent way to ensure you connect with your audience. For when they see you happy, surprised, sad, angry, disgusted, or fearful, they will be affected, making them more receptive to your message.

Emotions: How Will We Discover Them?

Emotion	Source of Emotion? (Complete the Statements)	< Select 3 and Give Brief Summary of What It Meant to Me (eg, a Lesson or Value)	< Select 1 and Explain What I'd Like to Convey to Audience (eg, a Lesson or Value)
Happiness	The happiest time of my life was…		
Surprise	The biggest surprise I ever had was when…		
Sadness	My saddest moment was…		
Anger	I have never been so angry as when…		
Disgust	I felt absolutely disgusted when…		
Fear	I have never been so scared as when …		

Emotions—Showing Them

I shall never forget the first time I competed in a Toastmasters Regional (Semi-Final) Contest. I delivered a great speech: it was thoughtful and different, well written and well delivered. I placed third. I couldn't understand it. Why? Where did I go wrong? With wounded pride, I turned to Cyril Crawford, a wise, old seasoned speaker in my club for an explanation.

In one short, unforgettable phrase, he put me straight—"You weren't sweating under your armpits." Translation: I didn't show my emotions about how I really felt about my message. The message was strong—but that alone was not enough to capture an audience for, as he explained, heart always trumps head.

Speakers who are less inclined to show emotion, be they Introverts, shy, or naturally low-emotional people, need to find ways to let what emotions they have come more readily to the surface. Let them be seen. The previous Table is a good starting point. The Table opposite follows from that. It offers a checklist asking you to think, before giving a speech, of how best you might express your emotions.

Consider facial expressions. Our face is our critical emotional signpost: smiling when happy; scrunched when unhappy; quizzical when uncertain; and sad when hurt. Consider the six primary emotions. If asked, you could readily "put on" an appropriate different face reflecting each emotion. The expression itself would signal how you were feeling, without a word being spoken. It follows that the clarity and intensity of each emotion can be magnified even further. Be guided by the possibilities shown at the bottom.

Once you have identified the emotions you wish to use, write them into your speech notes as seen in one speech by Vikas Jhingran:

.... (terror in my eyes, I look at my face in a mirror) *You've got to change this rule, mom* .... [Vikas in phone conversation with his mother who is selecting his bride in an arranged marriage. Vikas wants a "good looking" wife. His mother says they should be "comparable."]

Indeed, his speech planning is remarkable. Jhingran states that he writes his speeches with his desired audience's end of speech emotion in mind, ie, how they will feel at its conclusion. Consider that a long-term rather than a short-term goal.

Emotions: How Will We Show Them?

Emotion	Facial Expression	Breathing	Speech & Silence	Body Language	Energy & Movement	Audience Connection
Happiness						
Surprise						
Sadness						
Anger						
Disgust						
Fear						
Some Possibilities	Forehead & Eyebrows Eyes & Mouth Laugh or Cry Smile	Gasping or Gushing Heavy or Short Breathless Normal	Pauses or Silence Pace & Pitch Fast or Slow Loud or Soft	Confident or Diffident Speaking Height Arms & Fists Pondering	Deliberate or Uncertain Energetic or Pathetic Rapid or Slow Pacing or Still	Engaging or Serious Questions & Asides Dialog or Monolog Warm or Cool

Enthusiasm

If you aren't excited about your message, how can you expect your audience to be? Ben Franklin's observation simply states that if you want an enthusiastic audience, then you must be enthusiastic first. And the higher you ratchet your level of **Enthusiasm**, the higher the audience's is likely to be. Enthusiasm is contagious.

Another piece of wisdom from across the centuries comes from John Wesley, the founder of the Methodist Church, who told his preachers before they rode out on horseback in 18th century England: *Set yourself on fire with passion and people will come for miles to watch you burn!*

An audience today would likely describe an enthusiastic speaker as one with a sparkle in his eye; a warm smile; and an obvious belief in, or passion about, his message; whose words come from deep within—not just memorized and repeated from his head; whose faster speaking pace reflects his excitement; and who shows that he cares that we understand his message. It would certainly not be someone who is dreary, dull, or dour.

Another way to describe Enthusiasm is captured in its last four letters, *iasm—I am sold myself!* When you are sold on something, when you believe in something, your inner self glows as you share your passion for your subject. Dictionaries relate *enthusiasm* to words such as conviction, emotion, energy, excitement, feeling, fervor, fire, passion and zeal.

Reading quotations from enthusiastic speeches usually don't do justice to either the speeches or their enthusiasm. Therefore, this tool will offer only a few quotes. Instead, it will guide you to speakers on YouTube and TED to let you visually and emotionally experience Enthusiasm excellence in action. As you review the video links, look for the characteristics listed above.

Ralph Waldo Emerson gives us the bottom line: *Nothing great was ever achieved without enthusiasm.* That includes speeches.

Enthusiasm in Speeches

Can you remember a moment when a brilliant idea flashed into your head? It was perfect for you—Then all of a sudden, from the depths of your brain, another thought forced its way through the enthusiasm until finally it shouted, "YEAH great idea, but what if you—fall on your face?" [Falls on face] [01]

I did so much research, so much studying, and so much practicing, that my wife began referring to me as her roommate. I said—"Honey, this is the price I have to pay in order to live my dream." She said—"Go ahead, I just hope you wake up soon." You have to want your dream so badly that you become obsessed with it. [93]

One day I was watching TV and some crazy guy came on and said "Everything in life is arranged." And I jumped up and said "You better believe it." Now, wait a minute, Ladies and Gentlemen, don't tell me you don't argue with your TV—You know what the best part about it is—You always win because if you are losing you can shut if off and walk away. Then this crazy man carried on "Everything in life is arranged—Until you make it perfect." "What do you mean?" I shouted. ᵛᴶ

YouTube.com

On YouTube, there are two areas in particular with free resources to help viewers study and learn first-class speech communication skills:

1. Toastmasters (non-professional)

Simply type *Toastmasters* into your YouTube search box for a very wide offering. Typing *Toastmasters World Championship* in the search box will narrow the range down to an excellent sampling of top speech contestants in recent years.

2. Professional Speakers

If you type one of these three categories—*Inspirational Speakers, Motivational Speakers, or Professional Speakers*—into your YouTube search box, it will generate a remarkable list of known and unknown professional speakers, providing you a palate of speaking excellence. More often, however, it's likely you will enter the name of a specific platform speaker (eg, Tony Robbins) that you wish to view.

A Suggested Initial List to See Enthusiasm in Speakers

A global selection of Toastmasters and a style-diverse selection of Professional speakers follow. Each is different, each with his or her unique approach, each demonstrate the power of Enthusiasm. Enter these titles in your YouTube search box to access them:

Toastmasters

'A Sink Full of Green Tomatoes,' Mark Hunter, Toastmasters (2009, 7:29)

2013 World Public Speaking Champion Presiyan Vasilev (7:16)

Toastmasters Public Speaking World Champion 2015, 1st place (7:38)

Superb Storytelling—We Can Fix It—Manoj Vasudevan (2015-3rd, 7:56)

Toastmasters 'WINNING' Speech with Tony Robbins! (Andy Dooley, 8:00)

Professional Speakers

Zig Ziglar—Attitude Makes All The Difference (9:21)

Joel Weldon—Elephants Don't Bite! (3:51)

Charlie "Tremendous" Jones on the Price of Leadership (11:27)

Unleash Your Power—Tony Robbins (6:52)

Les Brown—You Gotta be Hungry [Les Brown Greatest Speech] (44:40)

Why America isn't the greatest country in the world anymore (6:00)—[Note this is an Enthusiasm speech from a movie]

TED.com

TED is an unbelievable source of great speeches from extremely diverse edge-of-envelope thinkers. TED's speakers are encouraged to focus on ideas worth sharing. They do, and their enthusiasm is infused throughout their speeches. So choose any (or all) of TED's All-time Top 20 Presentations to gain ideas about Enthusiasm in speaking. The link to their Top 20 is found in a Google search for … TED Top 20.

Exaggeration

Exaggeration is a grossly overstated or understated statement.

Its purpose is to ridiculously emphasize your point. Your exaggeration may be serious, amusing, or funny. It's a great way to add humor to your speeches and often is accompanied with appropriate gestures amplifying the exaggeration.

Consider this example:

Kurt Vonnegut uses adverbs with the frequency of an appearance of Halley's comet.

This description by Roy Peter Clark in his essential book for writers, *Writing Tools*, is a classic. It will be hard to create a more graphic exaggeration than this. But some speakers will—maybe even you!—and that's no exaggeration.

What follows is a selection of exaggerations, both overstated and understated, both amusing and serious. They show how all sorts of statements are tempting targets for your personal exaggeration engine.

And so began the development of my *alter ego*. Literally NO: Piano lessons—NO; High school debate team –NOPE; Graduate school - UH-UGH. <u>By the time I was 30, I had said NO more often than Toyota said "Recall."</u> [10-2]

As a kid, I was perfectly content having a rock as a pet. I had trained him to sit and stay. I wanted to teach him to roll over so he would gather no moss … I lost interest with my pet rock after I got married. My wife said if it was to stay in the house, it would require dusting every day or so. That became more work than I wanted to do. [JN.]

Bubba once told me that his best school year was his third year in 9th grade. [KS.]

For one second he let go. And she screamed—she screamed so, that the neighbor's, neighbor's blood froze. [04-2]

Given what we are hearing, has political lying entered an era of mass production?

God created the Ten Commandments and man has created 1 billion laws trying to say the same thing.

He has about as many money worries as Warren Buffet.

He has all the charisma of my ex-wife's lawyer.

He is one tough cookie: half German—half shepherd!

He lives in such a private community that even the police have an unlisted number.

He moved like a spastic pinball on amphetamines. [RH]

He must be very important—his office is the size of Rhode Island.

He's so optimistic he'd go after Moby Dick in a rowboat with tartar sauce in his pocket.

Her smile was wider than the Grand Canyon.

His home is so big it doesn't fit into a single zip code.

I grew up in a tiny tinpot town, a mere flyspeck on the map.

I had a job as exciting as an Excel spread sheet. [06-3]

I know the global financial crisis was bad—but this was really low budget! [10-3]

I live in a small SC town. I don't know about your town—but if it has a McDonalds, I am impressed. [WM.]

I looked up at Sam—who was as tall as a house! [04RH]

I was helpless. I did not know what in the world to do. I was quaking from head to foot, and could have hung my hat on my eyes, they stuck out so far. [MT]

I was so short in High School I used to pose as a bowling trophy. [KM.]

I'm living so far beyond my income that we may almost be said to be living apart. [EEC]

If (my mama) raised up to her full angry and elevated height, I thought I was looking at Shaquille O'Neal in a wig. [08]

In 1934, my Gran was about 16 months pregnant with her third child. [06-JE]

It was smaller than an ant's ankle, invisible to the human eye.

It's a slow burg. I spent a couple of weeks there one day.

It's as risky as jumping off a pancake.

Late at night, it got so frigid that all spoken words froze solid afore they could be heard. People had to wait until sunup to find out what folks were talking about the night before. [from the folktale *Babe the Blue Ox*]

My baby brother punctured my punch bag … it had been murdered! [06]

My boss was 50 shades of crazy. [15DW]

On many days, the dampness of the air pervades all life … envelopes seal themselves; postage stamps mate with one another as shamelessly as grasshoppers. [EBW]

Our first three months of Paramedic training?—Learning how to say "cardiac defibrillator!" [TC]

Our next speaker joined Toastmasters a gazillion years ago and is working on the Basic Manual for the nth time.

Picture your audience naked—that's just one of 4,279 suggestions I received from the folks back home on how to improve this speech. [03-2]

She had enough baggage to fill an airport carousel.

The English are passionate about breakfast, the only meal they know how to cook and which they will defend with their native weaponry–umbrellas and misaligned dentition. [CM]

There was a New York Philharmonic sound coming from my stomach. [RM.^]

There were more than a few milligrams of arrogance in him.

They are past their prime and time—just dinosaurs standing by a tar pit.

We went to a suburb of Calcutta, where the houses were so close sunlight was a myth. [07]

When I did something poorly, I got the full Harry Potter novel version—with the witch and broom included! [08]

Humor

Hundreds of books have been written on this special communication tool because of the warm welcome humor universally receives. My purpose here is to give you an introductory insight into what creates **humor**.

Most humor comes from a "Twist." Our minds are steered in one direction and then—Bam!—we find we are redirected down a different path, accompanied by our laughter due to the unexpected change in direction.

The Two-Part Twist is one statement followed by a misdirected statement, eg, *He was six foot—from shoulder to shoulder*. The Three-Part Twist (ie, a Triple) is the basic staple of comedians and follows this sequence:

First clause — <u>Sets</u> direction
Second clause — <u>Confirms</u> direction   [Pause]
Third clause — <u>Changes</u> direction   [The Twist]

A simple three-part (or three-step) example would be: *Jelly is a food usually found on bread, children, and piano keys!*

Allow your mind's funny bone to be tickled by the following:

Two-Part Twists

At first I didn't have much success with my resumes. After a while, I started renting out space on them to other job hunters. [JN.]

Can we be absolutely certain we are using 100% Extra Virgin Olive Oil? Is there some guarantee that a couple of those olives didn't go astray? [JN.]

Don't take yourself so seriously. The number of people who are going to attend your funeral is largely dependent on the weather that day. [97]

Each time I find a place that offers senior citizen discounts, I find a bunch of people in their Golden Years telling the person next to them ... "I'm on a fixed income," "I'm on a fixed income." Well, I want you to know in my case that is not true. I am on a declining income. And the only thing golden about the golden years is the gold I transfer from my bank account to the medical profession. [JN.]

Following instructions, I didn't eat any solid food that day; all I had was chicken broth, which is basically water, only with less flavor. [DB^]

I have a friend on the Police Force and asked him what he'd do if he had to arrest his own mother. [Pause]—Call for backup! [03-JM]

I have become a radical Baby Boomer [Pause] When I crossed over the 50-line last year I looked around for something that was good about being 50. [Long pause] I found absolutely nothing! [97]

I turned to run. Hit Sam Wilson's belt buckle right on the forehead—the Assistant Principal! As I lay on the floor looking up at Sam—he was as tall as a house—he leaned over and helped me up—by my right ear. [04RH]

In those days Internet connections were slow; it took hours to steal a good idea. [CM]

May I introduce you to my *alter ego*, Bob—Full name backwards—Bob [10-2]

My 401K Retirement Plan is so bad it's now a 104 K Plan!

My 9-year-old brother jumped in. He couldn't swim. I was very concerned. Not for him—for me. I'd have to explain it to my mother! [97-2]

My dad's favorite place to "shop" is on the side of the road. We now have four grills and three riding lawn mowers—none of which work. My dad keeps these on hand just in case he needs parts. [AD.]

My goal for this year was to lose 10 pounds. I have only 15 to go.

My mother always restated everything to be positive. I remember one report card. She looked at it. She looked at me. She said: I'm proud of you, son. I can see from your grades that you didn't cheat. [97-JB]

My mother was determined I would learn to ride that bike, even if it killed—me. [96]

The word "cereal" is from the Greek "ceres" meaning "Free Toy Inside." [CM]

This is a film that you can't watch just once. Your children won't let you. I've seen it 13 times since last Monday. [95]

Whenever I was asked if I had children my response was always the same: No—I work in a pediatrician's office! [96-2]

You have to want your dream so badly that you become obsessed with it. I said—"Honey, this is the price I have to pay in order to live my dream." She said—"Go ahead, I just hope you wake up soon." [93]

Three-Part Twists

At this point [an anxious father teaching his daughter to drive], I knew that to be truly effective as a driving instructor, you needed patience, perseverance, and valium. [DW]

I asked my friend: he said—Kwong, start your own business. I asked my uncle: he said—Kwong, go back to Australia. I asked my girlfriend: she said—Kwong, go away! [11-2]

It is as American as Hot Dogs, Apple Pie, and Political Scandals. [05LM]

Maybe you want a better voice—Reach out to a singer. Maybe you want better writing—Reach out to a writer. Maybe you want better tire-changing skills—Reach out—[long pause]—to me. [Pause] I'll give you Jesse's phone number! [13]

Now I'm not a boxer. I've had three fights in my life—and my sister won all three. [10-IH]

She liked outdoors; I liked indoors. She loved swimming; I feared drowning. She liked cooking; I liked to tell her how I missed my mama's cooking. [15-3]

The day our boy left home, my Soulmate stood at the end of the driveway watching his car, 18 years, and half our grocery bill disappear. [CM]

The ring was beyond sparkling, beyond beauty—beyond my budget. [TC.]

When someone isn't thanked, it's like a cake without its frosting, a car without its wheels, a Bud without its weiser.

Without music you merely exist—like a bear cub without its mother, like a shark in shallow water, like the ex Chief Accountant at Enron. [02]

Lines That Linger

One sign of a great speech is a phrase that resonates and remains with you. What grabs you may be its beauty, its originality, or its inspirational impact. Or simply, there was something about it that touched you. It's a phrase or **line that lingers** long after the speech is heard.

Following are some of my favorite lines—lines that lingered in my mind long after hearing them. Let them help you start thinking of what lines have impacted you and what you might craft to linger in your listeners' minds in the years ahead:

A candle was burning fervently for her in the cathedral of my heart. [SN.]

A man's character is seen when no one is looking.

A thousand difficulties don't deny the dream.

A war on a concept is unwinnable: poverty and drugs will never show up and sign a surrender document. [ZMB]

After putting the past back in the past I was able to play the game of life again. [10LC]

All know the way; few actually walk it. [BT]

And don't forget that if you win the rat race, you're still a rat. [KW]

Are we just allowing ourselves to be a group of has-beens and never-weres?

Are you the driver or passenger in your car as you drive through life?

As one person I cannot change the world, but I can change the world of one person. [PS]

Bad news doesn't call you in advance—it just knocks on your door at unexpected times. [MMc]

Boys, real men love for a lifetime, not for a moment. [04]

Don't cry because it's over—smile because it happened! [S]

Every child on earth is a treasure—it's just that some are buried. [96-2]

Few minds wear out; most rust out. [CNB]

Forget the thing that hurt you but never forget what it taught you. [CA.]

Freedom and equality are sworn and everlasting enemies. [WD+]

Friends are the family you choose for yourself. [11]

Have you ever been dream-jacked? Has someone ever stolen your dream? [CV]

Her laughter danced through the leaves like dappled sunlight. [07-RK]

How will I deal with him? I'll just give him a good ignoring.

How will you spend your year's allocation of non-refundable fragments of eternity? [CR]

I dream of unleashing a highly infectious virus of personal transformation that will reach every corner of the globe. [02-3]

I do not live in fear. I live in expectation. [GA]

I felt like that Pekinese dog floating around on a cushion of charisma [RC.]

I prefer tools, not rules. [RPC]

I thought I heard music, but it was just the rhythm of my heart. [10]

I wish life had an Undo function: private email sent to wrong person—Undo; getting a tattoo you can't show when you're sober—Undo... [10LC]

I'd been casting grandma to the margins of my life for years. [07-RK]

I'm not in a valley; just between two mountains. [GA.]

If you don't have a message you don't have the right to take up the audience's time. [CR]

If you work just for money, you'll always be underpaid. [CR]

In the theater of my mind I could see... [10MD]

Inspire before you expire. [15LF]

It takes no special talent to find an imperfection in another person. [05]

It's not what you've lost but what you have left that counts. [95-2] [quoting Harold Russell]

Just because you grow up doesn't mean you have to grow old. [97]

Man is but a strand in the web of life.

Originality is saying common things in uncommon ways.

Remember you are younger today than you will ever be. [01-EP]

She turned back to her work, and I am sure I heard her smile.[09]

Speeches don't have to be eternal to be unforgettable. [KM]

Stop traveling down the highway of your past. [12-DP]

The artist must often sail against the currents of his time. [JFK]

The greatest nation in the world? Imagination. The worst nation? Procrastination.[15EF]

The market for something to believe in is infinite. [HM]

The platform is the place where one-dimensional text becomes a three-dimensional experience. [MB]

The real question is not what is life but what is living? Are you living? [DD.]

The secret when faced with competition is not to compete but to create. [JW^]

The two most important days in your life are the day you are born and—the day you find out why. [MT]

Then I took that letter and tore it up until my hands were filled with a thousand paper tears. [91-PH]

There is no cast for a broken heart—there is no prosthesis for a shattered spirit. [94-2]

Though no one can go back and make a brand new start, anyone can start from now and make a brand new ending. [CB]

We could all tell a thousand stories, each adding nothing in itself but all adding up to something beautiful. [11]

We live but once; but if we live it right once is enough.

When my mama's sunset fell and turned to starlight. [04] [describing her death]

When you have a life of love, you will love the life you live. [15-RD]

Why be an "extra" in someone else's dream when you could *star* in your own? [PKP]

Why do we spend so much time exercising our bodies and not our brains? [12-3]

Worry is a wasted emotion. [SH]

You can't help the face you were born with but you can help the expression you wear on it. [94-3]

Memory Hooks

If they can't repeat it, they didn't get it! In that simple phrase, Patricia Fripp gives a critical success measure for our speeches.

When we are giving informational, persuasive, or inspirational speeches—where ideas need to be remembered—we have a responsibility to deliberately provide ways to help our audiences remember our key points and not leave retention to chance.

Elsewhere in your Toolbox, there are other tools that act as "**memory hooks**" such as the Phrase That Stays, Props, and Repetition. However, because of the vital importance of helping your audience retain the essence of what you are saying, here we introduce several additional approaches together with covering some other memory hook ideas.

Let's begin by imagining you are to give a speech on the five Great Lakes that divide the U.S. and Canada, and you want the audience to leave knowing what they are. One simple method is to turn the words you want remembered into an easy-to-repeat word or phrase.

In the case of the Great Lakes, HOMES is such a word and "Some Men Hate Eating Oranges" is such a phrase. HOMES reminds us of Lakes Huron, Ontario, Michigan, Erie, and Superior, whereas the phrase given allows the audience to readily remember the Lakes from West to East: Superior, Michigan, Huron, Erie, Ontario. In high school, you probably learned that this word approach is called an *acronym (pronounced akra-nim)*, and the phrase approach a *mnemonic* (pronounced ne-mon'-ic).

Another common example of *acronym* is SCUBA (Self-Contained Underwater Breathing Apparatus) and the *mnemonic* for remembering the first eight U.S. Presidents is: "Will A Jolly Man Make A Jolly Visitor?" (Washington, [John] Adams, Jefferson, Madison, Monroe, [John Quincy] Adams, Jackson, Van Buren)

Starting with words and phrases, more memory hook examples follow.

SMART

SMART is an example of a "word" trigger *(acronym)* sometimes heard in business— We need SMART goals: Specific, Measurable, Achievable, Result-based, and Time-bound.

OPEN UP

Timothy Koegel suggests that speakers develop a presentation style that is: Organized, Passionate, Engaging, Natural, Understandable (audience), and Practiced.

TEAMS

Some years ago, the target speaker in an Evaluation Contest was Glenda Teams. To help the audience (and me) remember the evaluation points I would focus on, I chose in advance five (5) speech qualities based on her name:

- Topic (message).
- Enthusiasm.
- Authenticity.
- Memorability.
- Summation.

I still remember Glenda's Caribbean Pirates speech and, yes, this approach won. And this approach will win for you in all sorts of situations. Speaking somewhere? Conjure up a word that relates to the organization or occasion and build your speech around it.

My Very Eccentric Mother Just Served Us Nectarines

Imagine being invited to give a speech on the Universe and needing to cover the planets from closest to farthest from the sun—<u>M</u>ercury, <u>V</u>enus, <u>E</u>arth, <u>M</u>ars, <u>J</u>upiter, <u>S</u>aturn, <u>U</u>ranus, <u>N</u>eptune. Yikes! Here is how a "phrase" reminder (*mnemonic*) can help. Such odd, concocted phrases are usually the best approach in speeches where you want the audience to remember a large number of points, particularly when they are in a specific sequence.

Providing An Historical Context

Ever had to give a speech (that is interesting!) on the history of Accounting? Or Michelangelo? Here's one introductory context idea that was used for both those speeches. *In 1492, Columbus sailed the ocean blue; two years later, Fra Pacioli, an Italian monk, launched his book on double-entry accounting, creating a new profession that has been in full sail every since.* In a separate speech on Michelangelo, the same Columbus ditty was be followed by ... *Friends, while Columbus was sailing, Michelangelo was quietly celebrating his 17ᵗʰ birthday with a few friends, reflecting on several great early works.*

The key is to link an unknown date or event to one the audience already knows, thereby providing a context for easier retention.

Providing a Date Context

"On July the 4th we got married. On America's Independence Day, I lost my independence." [15-3] [Note: If "And I haven't yet regained it in 17 years" had been added, we would have learned how long he had been married.]

An Easy-to-Remember Title

One of the great speeches in US history is Gen. Douglas MacArthur's *Duty, Honor, Country,* West Point's motto embedded in its coat of arms. Given to the graduating class, the relevant and well-known motto was the foundation of his 3-part speech.

An Easy-to-Remember Structure

One memorable speech titled *Crazy,* [02-3] in three parts, vividly described three characters we don't normally associate as being "crazy"—Abraham Lincoln, Mother Teresa, and Nelson Mandela. A well-structured, three-part format is a very easy way to make a speech memorable.

A Reminder in the Closing Words

The Aviators [10] an image-packed, powerful, poignant and emotional speech, had its message all drawn together for us to remember in its closing sentence: *Losing people is part of loving people—but if you do it right, they'll never leave your side even after they're gone.*

And, of course ...

Expressing an action-oriented (Think, Feel Do) message in simple, concrete words, and explaining *What's In It For the Audience*, always works, too.

Mental Musings

Hamlet, Shakespeare's most frequently performed play, focuses on thoughts and motives rather than action. Hamlet alone gives not one, but seven, soliloquys through which he shares inner conflicts—his **mental musings**.

The same concept is also very effective in speeches. Giving your audience a peek inside your mind—your inner conversations, conflicts, thoughts and musings—lets them understand what forces are really at work. In sharing your mental musings you are, in effect, having a side conversation with your audience, building and strengthening your connection with them.

This tool is not about delivering a Hamlet-like soliloquy. It's about providing a different dimension to your speeches—revealing your inner rather than outer self. For example, after the loss of his wife in the prime of life, one speaker poignantly shared his mental musings in these words:

> *But in the darkness of my misery*
> *I heard an insistent voice in my head.*
> *It said, "You can't quit on life—*
> *Not just for your own sake*
> *But for the sake of the one you lost.*
> *For she loved you for the way you were*
> *Not for the way you'd be if you gave in to self-pity.* [95-2]

The musings may be represented as an inner voice, your conscience, a discussion, or as an argument with yourself or another creature of your mind. It may be serious or lighthearted. And it can even be made fun for the audience if the "other voice" is presented as a character such as your *alter ego* (your second self), or your reflection, or even someone like Jiminy Cricket, Pinocchio's official conscience.

Often the musing is introduced with an alerting phrase like: an *inner voice*; *self-doubt rose up*; *my conscience whispered*; *I could hear my mother saying*; *I thought to myself*; *a little voice in my head*; or *it occurred to me*.

The following examples show how others have shared their mental musings:

Talking to One's Reflection

I looked over at the mirror next to me and it was as if my reflection stepped out of the mirror and walked over to me, and looked me in the eye, and stared me in the face—I told you I had a lot of conversations with myself. And I looked back at where the sun used to be and I said, "Wow, that was amazing. That sunset was one of the most beautiful things I've ever seen." But I had no idea that the sun goes down so fast.

My reflection looked at me and he said the three words I never expected to hear—He fixed me in his gaze and he said—"You're an idiot."

I said, "What?"

He said, "You heard me—You're an idiot."

I said, "Why am I an idiot?"

He said, "Because Craig—anybody's an idiot who thinks it's the sun that's moving." [99]

Some Mental Musings on a Flat Tire

I thought—I can handle it!
Loosen the nuts; place the jack down.

I saw the car going downhill. Bang!
The jack collapsed
The car collapsed
My lungs collapsed
An inner voice said—
"You are an idiot."
Then another voice—
"Reach—out."
Reach out?—
I can handle it.

Then that voice again
"Reach—out."
Reach out?
Should I involve them?—
Of course not.
Huh? [13]

Musings of a Man and a Dog!

While running, a small still voice asked a question: "How long are you going to be afraid?" At that moment I stopped—and decided I wouldn't be afraid anymore. I turned directly towards the dog and start running and screaming and hollering at him. The dog stops dead in its tracks, looks curious as if to think, "What manner of man is this that he would come chasing after a ferocious, barking dog?" [12-KRM]

Musings On an Arranged Marriage

Anjali was beautiful, educated and cultured. She was perfect for me—Or was she?—What if she was not the right one? What if I would have found the "Perfect Girl" if had I just waited—What if? [VJ]

Other Mental Musings

Actually in that moment I wanted to be better — I thought to myself, "Why did I have to have a total hip replacement? [11AT]

As I sat there preparing for that moment, the little voices in my head that speak to me, that are usually going at 10,000 miles per hour, they slowed down and all they said was—"You are not ready." [08]

May I present to you my *alter ego*, Bob. When I want to go forward my *alter ego* wants to go backwards. When I say Yes, Bob says No—And Bob always gets his way. [10-2]

I realized for the first time that I had lived my whole life like a postcard. Flat and incomplete. I had always been so busy building the future that I had never lived in the moment, the moment that had the smell, the touch, the sound and the emotion. The moment that is gone in a snap. Forever. Just like uncle Jay was gone. Forever. [07VJ]

Then I heard this voice and it said "Ed, if not you, then who?" I hate when this happens. I started to walk towards them. By the way, did I mention that he was tall? Six foot four, about 220?" [00]

Then self-doubt rose up to stare me right in the face. "Maybe you are a loser, James; maybe you are a failure; maybe you should give up." [04-3]

David Caban[99-3] titled his speech *That Little Voice*. It begins with David at 16 learning of a Talent Show. Should he enter? Here's where we first meet his two "little voices"— one in his heart and one in his head—and we listen to the dialog of these competing voices. His positive heart won on the Talent Show, but not always. Sometimes the negative, cautious little voice in his head won, with disappointing results.

Metaphors

A **metaphor** associates two things by depicting an idea, person, or thing in terms of something different that isn't literally possible. Consider these three metaphors:

> He has a heart of gold = He is kind
> He has a heart of stone = He is heartless
> He has the heart of a lion = He has strength of character

It's obvious what each of these metaphors means: each magnifies the image or attribute of what the speaker is wishing to describe as well as make it more vividly memorable.

Metaphors provide visual descriptions, eg, *He was trapped in a pit of despair*. Here, the image of a pit is used to create a picture of despair; isolation; darkness; and hopelessness. Of course, there is no such thing as a "pit or hole that contains despair," but this metaphor creates a vivid picture of what despair *means* and how it *feels*. It offers a fuller sense of what we are wishing to communicate.

In addition, a metaphorical image is often used as the theme for a whole speech, providing a powerful reminder of both the speaker and his message. At the 2007 Toastmasters International Convention, the keynote speaker, W. Mitchell, a former Marine, burn victim, and wheelchair-bound paraplegic, began:

> *How many of you in this ballroom this evening have been in prison?*
> *I ask that question of every audience to which I speak.*
> *I have...[been in prison]*
> *For this wheelchair was once a prison to me.*

By representing his wheelchair as a metaphorical prison we became acutely aware of the physical and mental anguish Mitchell once felt. He then continued his metaphorical theme throughout, describing how he escaped from it, and how we, too, can escape from our personal prisons.

Let the following examples of metaphors massage your mind:

Speech-Themed Metaphors

Stuck to a Bucket [94] is what happened to the speaker when his wet hand grabbed a bucket in sub-zero temperatures. Realizing, in real life, he was also stuck to a bucket (a job he no longer relished), he quit. Dropping the bucket (as he did) hurt; it tore his skin, but stronger skin replaced it. The same occurred in life when he quit his job. He encourages us to likewise let go of the freezing buckets of low-interest commitments that we are currently stuck to.

The speech *I Have A Gun,* [15DW] uses a graphic metaphor describing how, for many years, the speaker shot off deadly verbal bullets that wounded many around her—her mother, sister, friends, boss. It ends with the gun being put down.

The Ride of Life [04-3] depicts how our life is like a roller coaster ride with its ups and downs, flips and twists, and merciless uncertainty.

Scratch[15-2] is an engaging speech on how a car scratch can be polished out afterwards; so, too, can the verbal "scratches" (hurts) that we inflict on others.

In *The Train's Still Rollin'* [91] the speaker explains up front it's "a metaphorical train, a train that can transport you to success"

Phrase-Based Metaphors

A swamp of fraud and corruption...

America is a melting pot of nationalities, religions, and ideologies.

Are there empty chairs in your life ... those who need to be called back to the banquet of life? [10CR]

Armed with ignorance and bigotry, he attacked his enemy mercilessly.

Buried under an avalanche of debt.

But we refuse to believe that the bank of justice is bankrupt. We refuse to believe that there are insufficient funds in the great vaults of opportunity of this nation. [MLK]

Can the candidate inject the tired veins of the country's democracy with a modicum of courage and purpose?

Churchill mobilized the English language and sent it into battle... [EM]

Frozen in the ice of the status quo... [CR]

He returned from his travels with a suitcase of memories.

He was a quivering tower of jello.

He was an intellectual vacuum cleaner sucking up ideas everywhere he went.

He was in his favorite cigar shop—an island of tranquility in a sea of virility.

His statement makes the facts hostile witnesses.

I received a full bell curve of opinions.

I sat in my car and let the truth roll down my cheeks. [15JJ]

Ideas are the oxygen of progress.

In the courtroom of our conscience...

It was the echo of a disappointed soul.

The colors lit up the night and danced with symphonic grace and beauty. [AB.]

The elderly have sadly been airbrushed out of the picture of modern life.

The petri dish growing the culture for modern American society is not the schools, or the corporations, or even the family. It's the prisons. [SM]

The vision was tattooed on my mind.

Though interest rate temperatures were going down, the economy remained in intensive care.

We are entering an economic winter. [HD]

We are on a bullet train to bankruptcy.

What new ideas have taken residence in your mind lately?

You receive a passport to disfavor when you forget your anniversary.

You see, Grammie is living for the moment. She is scraping e-v-e-r-y last bit of peanut butter out of that jar of life ... and then licking the spoon! [15EF]

Parallelisms

Parallelisms are two or more balanced similar words, phrases or clauses in a consecutive grouping, indicating they are equally important. Listening to them gives you a sense that a symphonic balance has been added.

Consider the structural and auditory effect of these Lincoln examples:

Both read the same Bible, and pray to the same God. AL
The world will little note, nor long remember, what we say here. AL
With malice towards none; with charity for all; with firmness in the right. AL
We cannot dedicate—we cannot consecrate—we cannot hallow—this ground. AL

A selection of Parallelisms follow:

AIDS does not care whether you are Democrat or Republican; it does not ask whether you are black or white, male or female, gay or straight, young or old. MF

And the nation which disdains the mission of art invites the fate of Robert Frost's hired man, the fate of having "nothing to look backward to with pride, and nothing to look forward to with hope." JFK

Be sincere, be brief, be seated. FDR

Books are the carriers of civilization. Without them, history is silent, science is crippled, thought is at a standstill. They are the windows of the world; the engines of change; the lighthouses in the sea of time. BT+

Can you think of anything that wounds so deeply and lasts so long—as hurtful words? 04RH

Emotions feed the heart; facts feed the head.

Failure may not build character, but it will certainly reveal character. EH.

Freedom of speech will never be irrelevant, freedom of speech will never be obsolete, as long as you and I can look at the same problem and see different answers. BW.

From the dawn of creation ... each player makes his entrance, plays his brief part, and makes his exit. MJ.

God Himself is the Playwright, Producer, and Director of Life's Play. MJ.

Grim fate seems to be on the Red Man's trail—a few more moons, a few more winters. CS

I don't think we ought to waste any money, but I think we ought to do the job. JFK

I look forward to a great future for America, a future in which our country will match its military strength with our moral restraint, its wealth with our wisdom, its power with our purpose. JFK

I mean, the way I see it, to pass that kind of exam, you ain't gotta be white, but you sure better be right! EH.

I remembered the wonderful years I had spent with him when I was a kid ... his caring hug, his gentle smile. VJ.

I see men and women of great potential, and purpose, and promise. JD

I started trying to find something I could stamp on everybody I met—that little piece of goodness, that little piece of rightness. [05]

I was bedridden with depression, sick with anxiety. [10LC]

If it's right for us to dream as children, then it's just as right for us to dream as adults. [03]

If she pulls, you bend. If you pull, she bends. [15-3]

If we fail to capture the moment—the sound, the smell, the touch, and the feeling—what remains is a picture without a soul—a memory without emotion—just a postcard! [07VJ]

In that deep silence I heard the music of my dreams, the song of my talents, the symphony of my spirit. [07]

Let freedom ring from the mighty mountains of New York. Let freedom ring from the snowcapped Rockies of Colorado. [MLK]

Man holds in his mortal hands the power to abolish all forms of human power and all forms of human life. [JFK]

Most adults have forgotten—dreaming is fun, it's natural, and it's necessary. [03]

My grandmother woke me at 4:30am to do my homework all over again—and my handwriting had to be neat and legible! I wish she could see it now. It is beautiful and flawless. [14CA]

Never ignore inquisitive children. The longer you do, the louder they get. [03]

One moment, their eyes are dull and glassy. The next, they're shining with emotion. One moment, their skin is gray and waxy. The next, it's a glowing pink.

One moment, their body is stiff and awkward. The next, it's full of vitality. [JM]

Ours is not the choice whether or not we will accept the role—ours is the choice how we will play it. [MJ.]

The moment you made your entrance upon earth you began your journey into stardom. [MJ.]

The poem I read many years ago. The meaning I understood many years later [03-JS]

There is no caste for a broken heart; there is no prosthesis for a shattered spirit. [94-2]

This evaluation covers what I saw, what I felt, and what I heard. [MT.]

Veni, vidi, vici (I came, I saw, I conquered).[JC^]

We have no freedom when our minds are shackled to popular opinion, when our thoughts are manacled to mediocrity. [BW.]

We must be consistent if we are to be believed; we cannot love justice and ignore prejudice, love our children and fear to teach them. [MF]

We were cops and robbers, Cowboys and Indians, Barbies and Kens. [10]

We will not be satisfied until justice rolls down like waters and righteousness like a mighty stream. [MLK]

Yesterday is history, tomorrow is a mystery, today is a gift. [ER]

You campaign in poetry; you govern in prose. [MC]

You have to want your dream so badly that you become obsessed with it. It's all you think about—it's all you talk about. You wake up with it—you go to bed with it. You eat with it—you sleep with it—you drink with it. [93]

Pauses

Pauses are powerful. The pauses that occur when you speak naturally allow your audience to keep pace with what you are saying. In speeches, pauses can signal that an important point is to follow and/or an important point has just been made. They can be used to build emotion—ranging from dramatic effect to setting up a laugh. In serious speeches, they allow time for digestion and reflection. Pauses also play another role—they permit smooth transitions to a different mood or tempo at the end of speech sections.

Normal speaking pauses are sometimes classified as short (0.15 seconds), medium (0.50 sec), and long (1.50 sec) with dramatic pauses in the 3.0-7.0 seconds range. There are no fixed rules about length. What's right in each case depends upon you—your normal speaking speed, your experience level with pauses, and the impact you seek with each pause.

The four common methods used to indicate pause length in your speech draft are ///,—, <PPP>, and [Pause] with the number of slashes, dashes, or P's indicating your pause length. Some speakers use a mixture of all four.

Hamlet might have been a second-rate play if his main soliloquy had begun: *To be or not to be is the question I'm thinking about.* Instead, we react to his words when spoken as: *To be // or not to be? //// That is the question /////* where the pauses influence their meaning. Different actors have used different pause lengths thereby communicating different nuances. What pause lengths would you place in that sentence of Hamlet's? Pauses are as personal as your toothbrush.

Speeches populated by pauses have fewer words, but the audience is just as absorbed because of the meaning the pauses bring accompanied by the speaker's facial gestures. Presiyan Vasilev, Toastmasters 2013 World Speaking Champion, gave a pause-saturated speech. His spoken Words Per Minute were 78 compared to the average 128 WPM of 11 other recent WSC[B3], an amazing difference—yet it was a completely engaging speech.

Following is a cross-section of Pause examples to learn and adapt from:

Imagine you were born into a home with no books: how different would your subsequent life have been? [One speaker opened with that question, and paused for five (5) seconds for us to think about it before continuing.] [RW.]

Now that I'm free [after explaining break-up with his girlfriend], do we hang out together? Do we collaborate on projects? Do we have fun with each other? Absolutely <PPPPP]> not! (Laughter) [CV]

[Speech Opening] Ed Tate[00] stood quietly making comfortable eye contact with his audience before beginning. Such an opening pause usually adds attention to the speaker and makes the audience more anticipatory.

[Speech Close] I want to leave you with one thing today. This one thing is more powerful than anything I could ever say as a speaker. More meaningful than anything I can every say as a

Toastmaster. Ladies and gentlemen, I
want to leave you with this <12 seconds of
silence> Madame Contest Master. [99]

I have become a radical baby boomer.
When I crossed over the 50-line last year, I
looked around for something that was good
about being 50 <PPP >
I found absolutely nothing. [97]

[Speaker opens by looking at watch. <PP>]
In 2 hours and 47 minutes I'll be watching
TV<PP>
The Ohio State-Michigan game. <PP>
Mr. Toastmaster and Friends, <PP>
I'm a fanatic about Ohio State... [BB.]

We make commitments. <P> But do we
make them a priority? [OW]

And finally I asked. //
"Shelly/
Would you go out with me?" //
Her response was immediate //
It wasn't the one I had hoped for ///
"Me, go out with you? ///
Never." //// [10RD]

I have a dream // that my four little
children / will / one day / live in a nation
/ where they will not be judged / by the
color of their skin / but by the content of
their character. //// I have a dream today.
//// [MLK]

So let us begin anew //
Remembering on both sides /
That civility is not a sign of weakness /
And sincerity
Is always subject to proof ///
Let us never negotiate out of fear //
But let us never fear to negotiate //// [JFK]

Then it struck me. //
Like him /
I was chained by fears /
Waiting to die. //
No money /
Not really in love /
No achievement to be proud of. //
I was wasting my life //
And I knew it. ///
It wasn't until /
I could no longer touch Grandpapa /
That he really touched me. ///
It was as if I could hear him whisper //
"Here [touches his heart] //
Break free //
Break free, Son." /// [01-3]

I used to believe /
That to reach out was weakness //
I discovered my weakness /
Was in refusing to reach out. //
When you reach out /
You attract ideas /
That Lift—You—Up. //
When you reach out /
You attract solutions /
That Lift—You—Up. //
When you reach out /
You attract friendships/
That Lift—You—Up. ///
Maybe—you want a better voice //
Reach out to a singer ///
Maybe—you want better writing //
Reach out to a writer ///
Maybe—you want better tire-changing
skills //
Reach out—to me ////
I'll give you Jesse's number! /// [13]

Phrase That Stays

A Phrase That Stays (PTS) is a short phrase that summarizes your message or a key idea that is repeated during your speech for emphasis. It also helps its memorization. Similar terms used by speakers include the **Phrase that Pays**[DS], **Foundational Phrase**[CV], **Legacy Line**[RH], **Key Message Phrase**[PV], and your **Speech Bumper Sticker.**

Doug Stevenson describes in his excellent book[B1] the ideal attributes of his *Phrase That Pays*: it is short (6 words or less); it is positive (an emphasis on "do" rather than "don't"); it rhymes; it starts with a verb; and sums up your key point. He believes that audiences remember only one, or possibly two, points from a speech and this acts as a great memory hook. Examples taken from his keynote speeches include: *Look for the Limo, Get Over It, Pass the Power,* and *Flip The Emotional Trigger Switch.*

Stevenson's ideal characteristics are an excellent summary. Understand, however, that you can—and will—deviate from them and still be able to create a highly memorable phrase that audiences will remember and repeat.

The power of a Phrase That Stays is seen in three you probably know:

- *Just do it ...* Nike
- *15 minutes could save you 15% ...* Geico
- *Never leave home without it ...* American Express

The creation of your PTS begins with your message. What is the point you really want to get across to the audience? What do you really want them to remember? Let that marinate for a day or more and then start playing with possible phrases that capture the essence of your speech. Choose your favorite and thread it throughout your speech.

To loosen up your "Thinkery" consider the following phrases:

Accept the pain, reap the gain.

Act your wage. [DR]

Be a will-be, not a has-been.

Be different, not invisible. [CV]

Be prepared, not scared.

Be remarkable. [ET]

Be the rage of the stage.

Be the sage of the stage.

Be totally in.

Begin the journey.

Build a bridge—and get over it.

Build a habit hutch.

Change your game plan from success to significance. [BB]

Choose the pain of discipline over the rue of regret.

Choose to choose or you choose to lose.

Daily devote a dime of time.

Days are diamonds—let them dazzle.

Do 3 Daily Do-Its.

Do more, delay less.

Don't be scared, be prepared.

Don't compete—create! [JW^]

Don't die until you're dead. SS

Don't settle for greatness when you can be immortal. 04RH

Don't stop at the salad bar [there's a lot more beyond].

Dream it then achieve it.

Elevate the altitude of your attitude of gratitude.

Emails are for evenings.

Everyone deserves a second chance. 95

Fake it till you make it. TR

Flip the switch; brighten your day.

Follow your gut.

Forget the problem—find the solution.

Get up! 96

If it doesn't fit, you must acquit. JC

If you want it done get up with the sun.

Inspirate!—Don't motivate. RM.

Invest the time if you want to shine.

It's not about me DW.

Let your attitude reflect gratitude.

Life is a mission, not an intermission.

Light your candle at every man's torch.V

Live your legacy. RH

Live—don't give—your speech. RH

Make the effort. 15JO

Make your minutes matter.

Offer a choice, not an echo.

One step a day keeps failure away.

Paint in bold colors—not pale pastels.

Pay the pain, reap the gain.

Press the Play button of Life.

Raise your butt from its rut.

Savor your scars—stairs to the stars.

Say No—Be free to go.

Seek connection, not perfection.

Seize the hour—own the day.

Self discipline fixes most problems.

Sell the sizzle, not the sausage.

Shake your Welcome mat. HEF

Shine like a diamond. JB.

Speak to be remembered—and repeated. PF

Squeeze your own lemons first.

Stop selling. Start helping. ZZ

Stop stewing, start doing.

Success comes from sweat glands.

Success comes in cans, not cannots. JW^

Surrender to your greatness. DS

Take a check up from the neck up. ZZ

The first hour gives the power.

The pain passes—but the beauty remains. 87

The path to gain is pain.

Think next time, not last time.

Think solution—not problem.

To be free—just Be!

Train the brain.

Turn your scars into stars. RS

Turn your wounds into wisdom. OW

Venture out—don't veg out!

Wag more, bark less.

What got you here won't get you there. CV

Whatever you are be a good one. AL

When you snooze, you lose.

You become what you think about. EN

Your dream is not for sale. CV

Poetry Speaks

When poetic lines flow from a speaker's lips, audiences notice because such are rare, different, and apt. They can also be fresh, creative, and witty.

Verse, be it from a published poem or written to fit the speech, covers the landscape of emotions—from inspiration to fun, from *Desiderata* to Dr Seuss. A few well-chosen lines sometimes open a speech; more often they are used to summarize and close it. Sometimes they are used to both open and close a speech, as we heard in *A Scrap of Paper,* Larry Lands' touching 2001 WSC speech. He opened by taking a scrap of paper from his wallet and read five lines from Tennyson's *Ulysses;* five lines he had kept since high school.

> *We are not now that strength which in old days*
> *Moved earth and heaven, that which we are, we are;*
> *One equal temper of heroic hearts,*
> *Made weak by time and fate, but strong in will*
> *To strive, to seek, to find, and not to yield.*

The speech, interwoven with Tennyson's thoughts, focused on Lands' fascinating life, and concluded with an emotional restatement of just that short dramatic last line.

At the other end of the poetic Bell Curve, we find an apt, whimsical, self-composed stanza, delivered by Lance Miller in a contest speech.

> *Here lies Lance*
> *A victim of circumstance.*
> *Although he never quit*
> *He couldn't commit.*
> *He just tried and tried*
> *Until he died.*

Poetry, when sparing and appropriate, enriches and differentiates. The following are pieces I have heard in speeches. Let the poet within you speak!

Self–Composed for Speech

Music might not save the world
But it might save you
Music might not save the world
But it gives you something to dance to.
Music is not written
In the key of give-up
Music is not written
In the key of let-go
Music is not written in those keys—
Oh no!
Music might not save the world
But it eases the toils and strife
Because music is written
In the key of life.[02]
[Closing of a speech titled *Music in the Key of Life.*]

I don't know what life has to offer next
And it may be way out of line
But there is no reason
To fret and whine
For though you didn't cause
Your sorry plight
You do have the power—
To make it right. [VJ]
[Penultimate speech paragraph]

Whatever it is you love to do.
Pursue the passion that is in you.
It's a relaxing thing to do
And will build a better you.
It makes you glow and let you shine
How could it be a waste of time? [10JA]
[Speech closing]

Drawn from Popular Poetry

From Malloch's *Be the Best*:

If you can't be a highway,
Then just be a trail.
If you can't be the sun
Be a star
Because it isn't by size
That you win or fail
It's in being the best
Of whatever you are.

From Henley's *Invictus*:

I have not winced nor cried aloud
My head is bloody, but unbowed...
It matters not how strait the gait,
How charged with punishments the scroll,
I am the master of my fate:
I am the captain of my soul. [95-2]

From Lowell's *Cooper*:

I honor the one who is willing to sink
Half his present repute
For the freedom to think.
And when he has thought,
Be his cause wrong or weak,
Will risk the other half
For the freedom to speak.

From Edna St. Vincent Millay:

Heap not upon this grave
The flowers she loved so well;
Why bewilder her with roses,
That she cannot see or smell? [03-BW]

From John Greenleaf Whittier:

Of all sad words of tongue and pen
The saddest are these—
It might have been.

From Guest's *Sermons We See*:

I'd rather see a sermon
Than hear one any day;
I'd rather one should walk with me
Than merely tell the way ...
The best of all the preachers
Are the men who live their creeds,
For to see a good put in action
Is what everybody needs.

From e. e. cummings:

To be nobody but yourself
In a world which is doing its best
Day and night
To make you be like everybody else;
Means to fight the hardest battle [AL.]

From Nancy Wilson Ross:

No one saves us but ourselves
No one can, and no one may
We, ourselves, must walk the path
Teachers merely show the way. [TB+]

Fun Lines

He was such a very cautious lad
He never romped or played.
He never smoked, he never drank
He never even kissed a maid.
When finally he passed away
His insurance was denied.
Because the lad never really lived
They claimed he never really died. [CR]

Words from a paramedic—

You fall, you call,
We haul, and that's all. [TC]

Props

Props reinforce your message, show creativity, and provide a memory hook for your audience. They can be big or small, real or imaginary, commonplace or unexpected.

The prop that stands out most in my mind was one used by Bill Gates in a TED presentation—a jar of mosquitos. Holding the jar, he removed the lid and let them fly into the audience—highly effective for a speech on eradicating malaria.

In Toastmaster World Championship Contests, Morgan McArthur was the first to make a major impact with props. A veterinarian, he ended his speech about a special horse, titled *The Difference is Horsepower,*[93-2] by unveiling a full-size replica of it. His prop made a full-size point! In his following year's WSC speech, *Stuck to a Bucket,*[94] he used a shiny silver bucket as its central metaphor. He drew on an experience when, as a young veterinarian, it was so cold his wet hand stuck to a bucket, and used that physical and mental image throughout.

The following examples are offered to demonstrate the diversity of props used by speakers and to stimulate ideas for a future speech where you think a prop may be appropriate:

Imaginary Props

Brett Rutledge[98] has a brief but realistic imaginary laser sword fight (accompanied by all appropriate sounds) with his nemesis, Darth Vader.

In his speech about his *alter ego*, Robert Mackenzie[10-2] created an imaginary 10-15 feet tall prop by pacing out its dimensions and pointing up to indicate its height. In addition, when his *alter ego* took over, he opened its imaginary door and stepped inside, where the audience could see him mouthing words but not hear them. It was an unforgettable imaginary prop.

In a surprise twist, the reflection of Craig Valentine[99] steps out of the mirror and Craig carries on a vibrant to-and-fro conversation several times with this imaginary character.

Kwong Yue Yang[10KYY] is taught to hang onto an imaginary big red balloon, a metaphor for his big dream, to avoid being grounded by reality.

Rather than having a bicycle on stage, David Nottage[96] has us visualizing the bike he learned to ride by drawing on the usual associations: getting on, falling off, scraped knees, and pain-grimacing faces. He painted the whole humorous experience through our imagination.

When a couple divorces, blame flies freely. And the children often take sides, as Mark Haugh[00-MH] did when caught in this situation. He held up a finger, used it as an imaginary pistol and aimed it off-stage at his imaginary dad, counting out clearly: *Ready! Aim! Blame!* An imaginary pistol; an imaginary dad; and an imaginary bullet—of blame—was fired. It was highly effective.

Clothing as Props

Andy Dooley, giving a speech about meeting Tony Robbins at the top of a mountain is dressed accordingly—ski cap and goggles, red ski jacket and other outer skiwear.

Explaining the meaning of his attire with its local flavor earned David Brooks[90] applause as he satisfied the audience's curiosity about the Texas Tuxedo (jeans and a tuxedo) he wore.

In speeches two days apart, David Henderson[10] wore the professional outfits of the roles he was portraying. In the first speech, *Hope is the Best Medicine*, while wearing a white doctor's coat, with a tongue depressor and plastic stethoscope he talks of what he learned as a 6-year old "doctor" on his daily visits to his dying grandmother. In the second, *The Aviators*[10], he wears an aviator's outfit: a soft leather head cap, goggles, leather jacket, and even a white silk scarf. The outfit relates to Red Baron's air battle games he played as a kid.

Robed in a multi-color, full-length Ghanaian dinka, Albert Mensah[99-2] reminds us how we form impressions of others by what they are wearing. At the end, he removes his native formal attire to show his Western business suit and to stress his message—underneath we are all the same.

Visual Props

J. A. Gamache[01-3] emotionally and vividly described his grandfather's death—using a chair! He slowly tipped it on its back to represent Grandpapa's passing; the tip of one chair leg, representing Grandpapa's toe, was then touched lightly as JA said his goodbyes and thanks. It reminded me of God touching Adam's finger in Michelangelo's fresco in the Sistine Chapel. With just one simple prop, a chair, JA moved me twice.

Speaker used an overstuffed suitcase of interesting clothes and "things" which he drew from and spoke about. [RS.]

The stage is often co-opted as an prop by allocating parts of the stage to different people. Jonah Mungoshi[02-3] placed Mother Teresa, Nelson Mandela, and Abraham Lincoln, in different areas of the stage. Jock Elliott[11] did likewise, describing his three types of friends: (stage right) the friends of my blood; (stage center) the friends of my times; (stage left) and the friends of my heart. The speaker then points to each part when referring to the particular person.

With great enthusiasm, Robert Ferguson[98-3] bounded up a 10-foot stepladder for his farewell kiss at the open window of his girlfriend.

Other Visual Props Seen Used

$2 bill
Bicycle
Bonsai tree
Coconut
Cowboy hat
Financial Times (salmon-colored)
Hugely over-sized penny
Large black eye-mask
Large childhood photo
Letter
Light bulb
LP record
Marbles
Mirror
Nickels
Onion
Orange road cones
Rose
Trash Can
Whistle

Quips

At some time (often, many times) in our lives, we are called upon to chair or emcee a meeting; whether it be where we work, worship, or enjoy friendship and learning. The role of the chairman or emcee is not just to be serious but to add congeniality and a touch of lightness to the meeting to move it along more smoothly. That's where quips come in—short witty expressions that defuse tension, add smiles, relax attendees, or add an appropriate thought.

Quips are best when aimed at oneself, but also work well if aimed at another attendee well-known to the group and delivered with obvious goodwill and taste.

What follows is a diverse selection of quips to start your own personal Quip File so that your meetings run with a touch more levity and harmony:

Light Quips

A good speech is like a good pot of soup—it gets better when you reheat it.

A good storyteller is a person who has a good memory—and others haven't. [IC]

Cheer up—the worst is still on the way.

College tuition costs are getting so high that our kids' debts are catching up to that of small countries!

Comforting thought: Mark Twain tells us that no man is of such little value that he can't be used as a bad example.

Don't worry about the world ending today. It's already tomorrow in New Zealand.

Don't worry—if things get dull, oxygen masks will fall from the ceiling to stop you falling asleep.

Everything you hear from me is true—or would have been if it had happened.

He's been a member longer than Murphy's had a Law.

He's been here so long—long before the Dead Sea started feeling sick.

He's never had an unspoken thought.

He's so smart he could get a square meal into a round can.

His speeches are like pizza—even his bad ones are great!

I haven't lost my mind. Half of it just wandered off and the other half went looking for it.

I practice my speeches in front of my wife—which is okay—apart from her convulsive laughter.

I squeezed four years of college into six ...

I won't talk long—I am a short speaker

I'm retired. I was tired yesterday. I'm tired again today.

I've learned it's easier to send a man to the moon than win an argument with your wife.

If my memory gets any worse, I'll be able to plan my own surprise party.

Let's take a 5-minute break or else we'll have a 10-minute unscheduled loss of control!

Mark Twain says there are two types of speakers: those who are nervous and those who are liars.

Money talks—but for me it's usually saying goodbye.

My wife gave up shopping for antiques: she realized she married one.

My wife thinks I'm cool ... well, she says I'm not so hot.

My wife thinks that when I joined Toastmasters I joined a cult—I discovered she was right!

Now where was I before I interrupted myself?

Now, don't knock the coffee. You may be old and weak some day, too!

Remember monotone is the first 2/3 of monotonous.

Remember you're unique—just like everyone else.

Robert Frost told us that half the world comprises people who have something to say and can't, and the other half have nothing to say and keep saying it. We help solve both those problems!

Thanks for listening to my Longhorn speech—you know, that's the assignment with two widely separated points, with a lot of bull in between.

That speech probably sounded better in the original German.

That's a lot of one-handed clapping I hear out there! Now let's get serious and put both hands together.

There are 3 rules for creating humor—unfortunately I don't remember them.

Those were great words—well above my pay-grade.

To get us all in the mood, we're going to start this meeting with 15 seconds of your greatest fake laughing ...

Toastmasters are so supportive they clap even when they see grass growing.

We are a typical gathering: our average IQ is much lower than our average age!

We don't care how long you speak—provided it's said in a few words.

We want our evaluations to be so good that our club number will be carved on the face of Feedback Mountain.

Welcome to this special event where fun comes to be rejuvenated.

You only have to be within 50 feet of our next speaker to raise your IQ.

Thoughtful Quips

After a speech by Earl Nightingale a person gushed to him and said "I want to be a great speaker like you some day." Earl politely asked: "And what is it that you want to say?"

Any Toastmaster who doesn't get involved beyond club level is like someone stopping only at the salad bar—he misses out on the main course.

Don't be a phantom—one who leaves no fingerprints on our organization.

Few speakers are born with speaking skills. Emerson told us: All the great speakers were bad speakers first.

I don't know what brought you to Toastmasters but I know where it can take you. [DW]

If your goal is a trophy, go buy one. [DL]

Just because we follow a well-marked trail doesn't mean the people who marked it knew where they were going. [JJ]

People come to conventions because you can't hug old friends and shake hands with new ones over the phone or on Facebook.

Toastmasters take us on a journey from stage fright to stage delight.

Use what talents you possess: Henry Van Dyke observed that the woods would be very silent if the only birds that sang were those that sang best.

Radio Commentary

Churchill wrote in pauses, not paragraphs; each line ended where he took a natural pause. His speeches looked like short lines of poetry because he believed speeches, like poems, should be pleasing to the ear.

Here is the actual layout of just one sentence from a well-known Churchill speech:

If we can stand up to him,
   all Europe may be freed,
     and the life of the world
       may move forward into
         broad and sunlight uplands.

In paragraph format, the above would be: *If we can stand up to him, all Europe may be freed, and the life of the world may move forward into broad and sunlight uplands...*

Churchill's *pause* format made it easier to read (or glance at) as he roused Parliament or when he delivered his famous radio addresses to his countrymen (thus the apt term Radio Commentary. Understandably, the Pause Format is also used.) Now read out loud the following 7-minute speech set out as Churchill would. See how comfortable and helpful it is. Write your next speech in this format. It's unlikely you'll return to the *paragraph* method.

The Man With No Middle Name

Just a middle initial!
He was different in other ways, too.
He'd read the Bible—
Genesis to Revelation—
Before entering first grade—
And yet he's our last President
Not to have a college degree.
He's but one of five
To ever balance the Budget
And yet he holds
The lowest score ever in Presidential
   opinion polls.
His mother-in-law publicly predicted he'd
   lose re-election
Only time in all of history—
A mother-in-law was ever wrong!

Mr Toastmaster and friends
Harry S Truman—

My favorite President—
Not because Presidential Scholars
Rank him among our best—
Which they do—
But because he was one of us
A common man
Whom I respect and admire
For his
Character, courage and common sense.

He'd been raised with a reverence for
The Bible
The Constitution
And the lessons of History
Three forces that fused
To create his core character.

A **character** that caused him
To confront problems head on.
At the height of the Korean War
Truman fires America's most popular
   general.

Douglas MacArthur is publicly promoting
   we nuke Red China—
After the President had told him NO!!!
This firing ignites
Firestorms of protest.
Truman—stands serene
For history had taught him
The all-powerful, Roman Republic
   collapsed—in 49 BC
When its most popular general
Began dictating to its government.
He knew he'd made OUR republic safe.

Harry S Truman had character—
Annnnnnd—WAS one.
"I fired MacArthur
Because he refused to respect the
   authority of the President—
Not because he was a dumb SOB—
He was
But that's not against the law—
Not even for generals!"

As President
He was often vilified
For his courageous stands
Courage was never parked outside HIS
   Oval Office.
Years before the Civil Right Movement
He introduced a Civil Rights Bill
It lost
He introduced a Black Voting Rights
   Bill—It lost, too.
He insisted on integrating our armed
   forces.
That—he won.
Truman would always fight
For what he believed right
Win or lose.

But he never lost his small-town
   common sense values
He actually believed
He was elected
To do the right thing—
Not the popular thing.

Polls he pooh-poohed!
Aides once urged him
To take a poll-pleasing path
"Boys—tell me—
How far would Moses have got
If he'd taken a poll in Egypt?"

Like to see Truman at his best?
Then come with me—back to 1948.
Election Year.
Truman's up against a Dream Team.
His own Party—torn into three.
His campaign cash cupboard bare
Corporate chieftains come calling
Carrying checks—Big checks!

Truman throws them out—
Like Christ casting out the money
   changers—
For Harry S Truman devoutly believes
That America's most sacred site
Is—Our—Ballot Box
And he would NEVER sell that—
To any one—at any time—at any price!
He—would rather lose the election—
But he won.

My friends, our democracy has decayed
Since Truman's day
It has warped
Into vending machine democracy
Cash cascades into Congress
And the White House
And out pops the purchased legislation—
But this doesn't have to be!!!

DARE—WE—DREAM ...
That our next President
Will choose
To step into Truman's unfilled shoes—
Share his Character, Courage, and
   Common Sense
And restore to us the sanctity of OUR
   ballot box?
Knowing it has been done before
By a man—with no middle name. [BW.]

Repetition—An Introduction

The **repetition** of a word, phrase, or sentence in a speech emphasizes the word or idea, adds an ear-pleasing rhyme, or both. It is an effective tool that helps listeners remember your speech, as well as differentiate it from others.

Even in 7-minute Toastmaster speeches, repetition can be used effectively. In his WCPS speech, Dananjaya Hettiarachchi[14] repeated his title, *I See Something In You*, throughout his speech, often followed by an add-on: *but I don't know what it is.* In so doing, he created a two-part phrase, the theme of the speech. His repetitive phrase was not given in any consistent pattern such as at the beginning or end of sentences—it appeared wherever appropriate. Likewise, Darren Tay Wen Jie[16] in his semi-final speech, *I See Red*, managed to adroitly weave the word "red" into his speech 20 times!

Practicality is the only cap on how often a word or phrase may be repeated. In Martin Luther King, Jr.'s, *Dream* speech, *I have a dream* is repeated in eight consecutive paragraphs; then later, he repeats *Let freedom ring* in eight consecutive sentences.

The following examples show how Repetition has been used for both impact and listening pleasure. The special cases of Repetition at the Beginning or Ending of phrases or sentences, and Repetition in sets of three are the three tools that follow this Introduction.

Examples of Repetition

As I look at this audience, <u>I see</u> the concrete evidence of your hard work. And in this, <u>I see</u> an auspicious omen of the future. <u>I see</u> proud parents. <u>I see</u> loyal friends. But above all, <u>I see</u> men and women of great potential. [JG]

Belief in <u>progress</u> has faded. Many perceive technical <u>progress</u> as a danger, economic <u>progress</u> as a lie, social <u>progress</u> as a mirage, democratic <u>progress</u> as an illusion. [MP^]

But she threw me in that water, time and time and time again. [08]

Different things strike different people in different ways. [WC]

Doubt whom you will, but never doubt yourself. [CNB]

Grandpa's favorite day was when he met Grandma. He was faithful in his life to <u>one</u> wife, <u>one</u> job, <u>one</u> God. [RH^]

Harriet Tubman had intelligence, grit, and determination. <u>But that's not what made her great</u>. She achieved success by winning her personal freedom. <u>But that's not what made her great</u>. <u>What made Harriet Tubman great</u> was that she went back, took others by the hand and conducted them along the road to freedom. [97-SZ]

I am no longer acquiring things. I am acquiring experiences. [15GA]

I get so wrapped up in what I need to do, what I plan to do, what I want to do that I forget about the other person. [DW.]

I've had good days and bad days and going half-mad days. [JB]

I learned that when you have a dream deeply rooted in your heart, failure can humiliate you, and failure can frustrate you, but failure cannot stop you. EH.

I no longer get phone calls from my mother. I no longer get phone calls from my brother. 13RS

If everyone helps, everyone wins. 15-JJ

If you can't readily repeat your Mission Statement you don't have a Mission.

It was we, the people; not we, the white male citizens; nor yet we, the male citizens; but we, the whole people, who formed the Union. And we formed it, not to give the blessings of liberty, but to secure them; not to the half of ourselves … but to the whole people, women as well as men. SBA

My life began to play out like a movie—
Smoke began to fill the floor,
A light from the window shined on his face,
And choirs of angels began to sing. 16DB
[The last 3 lines were amusingly repeated 5 times through the speech, each time she fell in love.]

The tragedy is not that things are broken. The tragedy is that they are not mended. AP

There is a difference between people who live in the future and people who live in the pasture. The difference is horsepower. 93-2

We're working to get the right things done, for the right people, and for the right reasons. JW

When Jackie fell and hurt her elbow, It seemed like no big deal at first. She took too long getting back up. No big deal.

Her arm took too long to heal. No big deal. Until the doctor said she had a bone infection. That was a big deal. The reason why was even bigger. Jackie had sickle-cell anemia, which meant our flying days were over. 10

When we lack competition, we lack greatness. BR

Words have power. Words are power. Words could be your power. You can change a life, inspire a nation, make this world a beautiful place. 15

The Special Case of Reverse Repetition
[Where a statement is turned around for ear-catching effect.]

Ask not what your country can do for you, but rather what you can do for your country. JFK

I had changed everything in my life—but nothing had changed. I still felt I was going nowhere. 05

I meant what I said and I said what I meant. S

I wanted to leave my job—but I didn't want my job to leave me. 09-CK

Now this is not the end. It is not even the beginning of the end. But it is, perhaps, the end of the beginning. WC

The music of our lives and the life of our music are woven into the fabric of our being. 02

Though no one can go back and make a brand new start, anyone can start from now and make a brand new ending. CB

When you change the way you look at things, the things you look at changes. WD^

Repetition—As a Sentence Beginning

Repetition in a speech is a powerful emphasis builder and ear pleaser. When it occurs at the beginning of a series of consecutive phrases or sentences both characteristics are magnified. It has been a favored tool of speakers throughout history.

As you read the following examples you will sense the strength that comes when repetition opens a series of clauses or sentences. It's easy to do.

There was a sound of laughter …
There was a wit …
There was a man …
There was a father …
There was a husband … [MM]
[The above descriptive phrases opened the first five short paragraphs in a eulogy of President John Kennedy.]

A 6-year-old struck down by polio—
Braces, confinement, excruciating pain.
Each doctor's visit she asked—
When can I take my braces off?
When can I walk?
When can I play with friends?—
I don't know. Maybe never. [87]

Eons ago—humans did not own the lands in the North Country.
Eons ago—people lived off the gifts that the land offered them.
Eons ago—lived a man known as the Sky Painter [AB.]

Fight the enemy from within.
An enemy of low self-esteem
An enemy of hopelessness and despair
An enemy of drug abuse—
An enemy that plagues our communities. [KM]

He drank.
He drank until he forgot.
He drank until his children were taken away.
He drank until he lost everything. [07-DK]

I let go of my fears;
I let go of the expectations;
I let go of the perceptions;
I let go of what other people were telling me to do or what to be,
And I let go of what they thought of me. [16JL]

I was committed to be a jet pilot.
I will NOT be defined by his words!
I will NOT be defined by my doubts!
I will NOT be defined by his pink slips!
—I worked even harder. [06-2]

The lights…turned the Sky Painter into a wolf.
As a wolf, he could travel and bask under the beauty of his creation.
As a wolf, he would remain alone.
As a wolf, he would be feared [AB.]

It means you're not just here to inform.
It means you're not just here to entertain.
It means you're not just here to persuade.
Those little pixels on the computer screen can change somebody's life. [JM]

I immediately thought only of the things that she would never do:
She would never know the feeling of love's first kiss.
She would never hold the hand of a boy who would take her on a date.
She would never know the thrill of graduation and looking forward to college.
She would never hope for the day of a wedding and a honeymoon.

She would never know a home other than that she shares with her sister.
She would never discover the news of a new life growing within her.
She would never hold her own child in her arms. KT
[Upon learning his beautiful 9 year-old had 9 weeks to live]

Maybe because I am about to turn 30.
And maybe I don't have the doctor husband with the perfect teeth—or the 2.5 kids.
And maybe I did burn my eyelids at the lake and have 2 new wrinkles.
And maybe I'm in the middle of my latest mid-life crisis.
But I DO have ... RR.

My mom's voice goes two octaves higher.
She smiles,
She squints, and
She squeals out, "Oh, thank you!"
Regardless of the gift. 16KH

My parents "comforted" me with
"I told you so."
"I told you not to quit your job."
I told you so.
"I told you not to waste your time."
I told you so.
That week that's all I heard. 14-2

Now you are free.
Free of the pressure of exams.
Free to begin the next stage of life and
Free to pay back your student loans. KA

Tonight is not too early.
Tonight is not too late.
Tonight is the perfect time
For YOU to live your Legacy. RH.

Our red-headed second President
With his blueprints was...
An architect of buildings,
An architect of our nation,
An architect of our freedom. BW.

Today John Fitzgerald Kennedy...
Lives on in the immortal words and works that he left behind.
He lives on in the mind and memories of mankind.
He lives on in the hearts of his countrymen. LBJ

We rushed around looking for the new insurance cards.
We rushed to change clothes, and
We rushed to the hospital. DW.

We shall not flag or fail.
We shall go on to the end,
We shall fight in France,
We shall fight on the seas and oceans,
We shall fight with growing confidence and growing strength in the air,
We shall defend our Island, whatever the cost may be,
We shall fight on the beaches,
We shall fight on the landing grounds,
We shall fight in the fields and in the streets,
We shall fight in the hills—
We shall never surrender. WC

When I see tourists looking at a map,
I offer them directions.
When I see a tour bus,
I wave.
When I drive through a toll booth,
I pay for the people behind me. 16SF

We will always remember.
We will always be proud.
We will always be prepared
So we may always be free. RR

Repetition—At Sentence Ending

A word or phrase repeated at the *end* of a clause or sentence creates greater emphasis than at the beginning because the natural pause that follows allows us to think about what was said. Further, the natural pause at the end of a sentence is longer than at the end of a clause, making it the more powerful of the two.

My favorite example of end-of-sentence repetition was delivered over 150 years ago by Harriett Tubman, an illiterate, escaped slave who helped other black slaves to freedom via the Underground Railroad.

If you hear the dogs, keep going.
If you see the torches in the woods, keep going.
If there's shouting after you, keep going.
Don't ever stop. Keep going.
If you want a taste of freedom, keep going.

Even today, we can feel her pulsating passion rising as she keeps repeating "keep going" at each sentence's end. Let the foregoing and following inspire you to master this unique tool to use in one of your upcoming speeches:

...And so she took a ring from her finger and placed it in his hands. [MM]
[The sentence above closed the first five short paragraphs in a eulogy of President John Kennedy.]

For no government is better than the men who compose it
And I want the best
And we need the best
And we deserve the best. [JFK]

Hear no evil. See no evil. Speak no evil.

Hold my hand;
Hold my hand;
Squeeze my hand. [04-2]

I have fought against white domination—
And I have fought against black domination. [NM]

I have promises to keep,
And miles to go before I sleep,
And miles to go before I sleep [RF]

I took hold of her hand,
And I said, "Yes."
And it felt good.
So I did it again.
A child - YES;
A new business - YES;
A second child - YES;
A 30-year mortgage - YES;
A third child - UH, YES;
Toastmasters - OOH . . . Yeah.
Twenty years a world of YES [10-2]

If you believe
You are safe from AIDS
You are in danger.
Because I was not hemophiliac—
I was not at risk.
Because I was not gay—
I was not at risk.
Because I did not inject drugs—
I was not at risk. [MF]

From Made in China,
To Designed in China,
To Imagined in China.

Let us not speak of darker days;
Let us speak of sterner days. WC

Men have never been good.
They are not good.
They never will be good. KB

Take whatever idiot they have at the
top of whatever agency and give me a
better idiot.
Give me a caring idiot.
Give me a sensitive idiot.
Just don't give me the same idiot.
[Frustrated Hurricane Katrina official]

The greatest leader <u>of our time</u>—has been
struck down by the foulest deed <u>of our
time</u>. LBJ

The President presents
The State of the Nation;
The people ponder
The Fate of the Nation. TF

The time for the healing of the wounds
has come. The moment to bridge the
chasms that divides us has come. NM

Then I'll be all aroun' in the dark. I'll be
ever'where—wherever you look. Wherever
they's a fight so hungry people can eat,
I'll be there. Wherever they's a cop beatin'
up a guy, I'll be there … An' when our
folk eat the stuff they raise an' live in the
houses they build—why, I'll be there…" JS

There is no Negro problem.
There is no Southern problem.
There is no Northern problem.
There is only an American problem.
And we are met here tonight …
To solve that problem LBJ

There is nothing wrong with America
that cannot be cured by what is right with
America. BC

We are born to sorrow
Pass our time in sorrow
End our days in sorrow

We here highly resolve that these dead
Shall not have died in vain …
And that government
Of the people
By the people
For the people
Shall not perish from the earth AL

When I was a child
I spoke as a child
I understood as a child
I thought as a child B

Whether that dream is to
Invent something
Start something
Build something, or
Create something—
It all starts with a good education MR

What lies behind us
And what lies before us
Are tiny
Compared to what lies within us. RWE

With this faith we will be able
To work together,
To pray together,
To struggle together,
To go to jail together,
To stand up for freedom together—
Knowing that we will be free one day. MLK

You want this outcome
I want this outcome
We all want this outcome—
Let's work together and achieve it.

Repetition—In Sets of Three

Words, phrases, or ideas repeated in threes stand out because they incorporate the characteristics of **Triples** (q.v.): a sense of balance, completeness, and auditory pleasure. The repetition emphasizes all three, especially when your inflection alters with each repeated word or phrase, such as:

Are you ready?—Are you ready?—ARE YOU READY? [VJ]

Likewise, using three different but similar-meaning words to describe an idea focuses on, and magnifies, the idea as this well-known line from Lincoln's *Gettysburg Address* illustrates:

We cannot dedicate, we cannot consecrate, we cannot hallow this ground.

The words *dedicate*, *consecrate* and *hallow* all have similar meanings reinforcing the sacredness of where they were.

Be inspired by the following to repeat a word or idea three times in speeches.

Repeating of 3 Words or Phrases

Better listening.
Better thinking.
Better speaking
[Toastmasters® Founding Motto]

But isn't that where it all begins?
The classroom—
The standardized test
The standardized desks
The standardized standards? [03-2]

He was always late—
Late for work
Late for appointments
Late to pay our bills [14-2]

I learned that your mind can—
And will—
Amaze your body if you just keep
Saying to yourself—
It's possible.
It's possible.
It's possible.[93] [Speech ending]

If I just had more time.
If I just had another opportunity.
If I just found something new [01]

As Les Brown said, "I was sick and tired of being sick and tired." I had a dead-end job, a dead-end relationship, and a dead-end life. Ladies and gentlemen, I needed help. [99]

Do I want to fit in—or do I want to stand up, stand out, and stand fast—for who and what I am? [09]

Every day when school was over, his father would wait in a bright shiny BMW to pick him up. And there I was waiting, waiting, waiting for my dad to pick me up. [12-2]

Government of the people, by the people, for the people, shall not perish from the Earth. [AL]

I have three best friends and here they are: (move to stage right) the friends of my blood; (move to stage center) the friends of my times; (move to stage left) and the friends of my heart. [11]

I wanted to grow up to be just like the Lone Ranger. I wanted to ride a fiery white stallion and wear a mysterious black mask. And I wanted to shoot silver bullets. [90]

My brother [RFK] need simply be remembered as a good and decent man, who <u>saw</u> wrong <u>and tried to</u> right it, <u>saw</u> suffering <u>and tried to</u> heal it, <u>saw</u> war <u>and tried to</u> stop it. [EK]

Now I'd seen my mama cry before. But Mothers cry three kinds of tears: tears of joy, tears of sorrow, and tears of shame. [14]

So my dad introduced me to this strange club, that had a strange name, with strange people. [14]

When we cease to be challenged … and we don't do something about it, we are frozen—Frozen because we are afraid to change; frozen in a hell of our own choosing; frozen alive. [94]

Expressing 3 reinforcing ideas
[Expressing an idea three ways]

Ask yourself this:
Is there anyone out there I have not yet let go?
Is there anyone out there I have not yet forgiven?
Is there anyone out there I have not yet set free? [CV]

Americanism is a question of principle, of idealism, of character. [TR^]

But Kennedy's serious purpose was to acknowledge, to praise, to reinforce, the endurance and the fighting spirit of those people. [95-2]

Friday, the previous day, I was hopeless, I was defeated, I was fired. [04-3]

Friends, in life it doesn't matter so much whether we arrive at a 5-star hotel or at a cow paddy; what matters is that our minds are free—Free from despair, worry and regret. [10-3]

I guarantee you that the other 23 hours and 55 minutes of your day will be filled with tranquility, serenity, and a peacefulness you never knew even existed. [99]

I then began preparing to enter the International Speech Contest. I did so much research, so much studying, and so much practicing, that my wife began referring to me as her roommate. [93]

I was told there would be no Mt. Everest too high, no Grand Canyon too deep, no Sahara Desert too wide, if I could live in one thousand, four hundred forty minutes—the number of minutes in a day. [11AT]

In our lives there are plenty of naysayers, doubters, can't-be-done specialists. [93-2]

It was a letter rich in memories—a letter of recognition, of appreciation, of gratitude. [03-BW]

It was Christmastime—a season of love, cheer, and goodwill. [95]

My faith in the Constitution is whole, complete, total. [BJ] [Watergate Hearing]

She said, "Robert, I see something in you—you are 35, you are going nowhere, and you're broke. Yet I believe in you, I have faith in you, and I want to spend my life with you." [10-2]

The future is not meant to be pot luck, blind chance, pure fate. We make our own decisions. [94-3]

Truman devoutly believed that America's most sacred site is the ballot box and would never sell that to any one, at any time, at any price. [BW.]

You only live once. One time. There are no "do-overs." [15MQ]

Rhyme

The ear loves rhyme and rhythm, both in song and speech. They make listening pleasurable. Think of the nursery rhymes, with their singsong rhythm, that you recited so readily and easily as a kid. When you add rhyme to your speeches, even adult audiences enjoy that melodic touch, too.

Rhyme can come from just two words. Weaving *three* rhyming words into a speech makes a noticeable, memorable difference.

From Dr. Seuss, one of our great rhymesters, in *Horton Hatches the Egg,* see how he makes two lines memorable through their unlikely rhyming last words:

"I meant what I said, and I said what I meant...
An elephant's faithful—one hundred per cent."

Read the following examples out loud. Let the rhyming words roll around your tongue. Hear their music and observe how easy rhyme can be created. Then start experimenting with your own rhyming phrases, threading them into your speeches to add pleasure to those who hear you speak.

Acting as rulers who neither have to explain or restrain themselves

And the fantasy will never become reality [95]

At this end of the Bell Curve resides an erudite hermaphrodite.

Automate or liquidate

Chi-chink! Chi-chink! I had plenty of ink! [05]

Digging deep into the history and mystery of life ...

Do you want education or validation? [CV]

Don't fret and regret.

Don't remain in your prison of pain.

Either sizzle or fizzle.

Faith without might is futile and might without faith is sterile. [RN]

Four score and seven years ago... [AL]

From know-how to nowhere

Gratitude is the attitude that helps you dial your life up. [15-JJ]

He went from elation to deflation.

I faced fear, depression, and thoughts of repossession. [04-3]

I had fulfilled my dream: the answer is not in that magic pill—or with Dr. Phil. [07]

I want to put a song in your heart, some glide in your stride, and some hump in your bump. [02]

I was screaming and bawling—the hounds were howling and circling. An ugly one-eyed dog clawed and scratched his way onto the trunk, his yellow teeth snapping and foaming. [04]

If you do the crime, you do the time. [JJ]

In the West, history, philosophy, literature, art, even religion, have only succeeded in sociologising, psychologising, relativising, socialising, Freudionising, secularising, materialising, immonentising, almost dehumanising themselves [CM+]

Injustice anywhere is a threat to justice everywhere. [MLK]

Is it not astonishing that, while we are plowing, planting, and reaping ... erecting houses, constructing bridges, building ships, working in metals ... while we are reading, writing, and ciphering ... we are engaged in all the enterprises common to other men. [FD]

It was tempting, but I resisted the temptation and enjoyed the relaxation. [14-3]

It's not about me—it's about we. [15WK]

It's the reason for the season.

Language happens because human beings are desiring machines. [SL^]

Licking and sticking Green Shield stamps

Living with Andy took me from manhood to motherhood. [14-2]

My parents, having tried everything—from tutoring to mentoring, pleading to threatening—turned to the supernatural. [07]

One hundred years later, the life of the Negro is still sadly crippled by the manacles of segregation and the chains of discrimination. [MLK]

Some call it illusion and magic. I call it collusion and tragic.

Strangulation by regulation

That day, my numbed numbers-trained brain finally figured it out! [BW.]

The American economy is like a bicycle; when it stalls, it falls. [KR]

The beauty of the Blues is that it shows us that we can take our hardest of hard times, our saddest of sad times, add a little waa-waa and some ka-ching and create a tune that can make your heart sing. [02]

The more personal your speech, the more universal its reach. [MMc]

The ship started to sail and I said, "Say, goodbye, Wi-Fi." [14-3]

There is despair, Mr President, in faces you never see, in places you never visit. [MC]

There's so much to gain by being Jane. [10-3]

They forgot we weren't connected to a hot spot. [14-3]

We can never be satisfied as long as ... [we Black people] ... cannot gain lodging in the motels of the highways and the hotels of the cities. [MLK]

We have now arrived at Dysfunction Junction.

We want to thrive, not just survive.

Winners and sinners

With dexterity and flexibility

Rhyme in Threes

A dentist drills, fills, and bills.

From care-worn to carefree to careless

Go out—with a dash, a splash, and panache.

He was harmless, charmless, and soulless

His leadership style is one of belligerence, arrogance, and ignorance.

It's Shanghai, Mumbai, or Goodbye!

Make them high. Make them cry. Make them try. [96]

Martin Luther King's dream of a world without racism, militarism, and materialism remains a distant dream. [JW+]

They were a sorry bunch—pale, male, and stale.

Roasts

Roasts are fun! They are special gatherings to humorously honor a special person. Their purpose is to make good-hearted fun of the honoree without embarrassing him (or her). Much of the humor aimed at the honoree has a slender connection to reality, which is then generously exaggerated.

In preparing your Roast, start by identifying various characteristics of the honoree such as his or her job, interests, habits, age, physical characteristics (eg, build, height, looks), background and marriage. Choose 3-4 of those characteristics that appeal to you most, then research and create a series of related, often one-line jokes surrounding each of them.

New Roasters usually find preparation easiest by reading a book of one-liner jokes identifying those that relate to the Roastee's characteristics. Seasoned Roasters continually build their own personal collections that can be readily adapted to the specific honoree each time they are called upon to roast another friend.

What follows is a cross section of such lines that you, when next called upon, may borrow and adapt to "honor" your honoree. Add those lines that resonate to start your own personal Roast file. Fun is on the way!

After 28 years of marriage, Dan and Daisy have figured out the secret to a happy marriage. Two times a week they go to that beautiful French restaurant, Dominiques, to enjoy some great food and wine. Dan goes on Tuesdays; Daisy goes on Fridays.

As a youth, he spent a fortune on deodorant. That was, of course, before he realized people just didn't like him.

As one friend explained, he's a modest little person—with much to be modest about.

Dan believes that money isn't everything—but says it sure keeps his kids in touch.

Dan believes the only two things we do with greater frequency as we get older are urinate and attend funerals.

Dan finally got around to writing his first book and sent me a copy. Of course, I dropped him an encouraging note: "Dan, from the moment I picked up your book until I laid it down, I was convulsed with laughter. Some day I intend reading it."

Dan gets most of his news from TV. Says he reads the paper occasionally—depends when his neighbor is away.

Dan has the right balance abut life. Last month he bought a $2,000 riding lawn mower and this month a $1,500 exercise machine for the basement!

Dan is a great dancer. You should see him on the dance floor. His favorite dance step is the Sinatra—he does it his way.

Dan is always complaining about his workload. Says he does the work of three men. He didn't tell me they were Larry, Curly and Moe!

Dan is an ultra-cautious guy—even when reading health books, he fears he may die of a misprint.

Dan is one of those guys who is not overwhelming, not underwhelming—just whelming.

Dan is so curious he's like a wandering verb in search of a noun.

Dan is so religious he has stain-glassed contact lens.

Dan keeps changing his mind so much, his website is *weathervane.com.*

Dan married well. His wife has the face for TV. He has the one for radio.

Dan says he doesn't feel old. In fact he doesn't feel anything until noon. Then it's time for his nap.

Dan should have been an actor. He could easily have be an extra in *One Flew Over the Cuckoo's Nest.*

Dan sometimes shows his sharp mind. Recently, he witnessed an accident. When the police asked him who caused it he paused, then replied: Well, I can't be certain—both cars got there at the same time!

Dan sometimes suffers from seizures—of common sense.

Dan's abilities are closer to Donald Duck's than Donald Trump's.

Dan's an antique collector—he has one of the most extensive collections of old unpaid bills I've ever seen.

Dan's gene pool doesn't have a deep end.

Dan's luck is so bad that if he bought a cemetery, people would stop dying.

Dan's occasional flashes of silence are what make his conversations so delightful.

Dan's plan to change the world seems to have been airbrushed from history.

Dan's so secretive he even writes Confidential on the postcards he mails.

Did you know Dan is multilingual? Yes, he knows 3 French words—*cul de sac.*

Everything I tell you today about Dan is true—except for the stuff I make up!

Fortunately, as Dan got older, the law of averages began to work for him—nobody can be that stupid forever! Which just proves that the porch light must turn on sometime!

I admire Dan's self control. He can resist everything—except temptation.

I have been impressed with how Dan has always been thinking of ways to make money. Even when he was young and poor he used to shake two dimes together in his pocket hoping they'd mate.

If there's any mistake Dan hasn't made, you can bet he's working on it.

In his younger days Dan is most proud of being selected as one of the 10 Best Looking Men in Ohio—by the Ohio Blind Association.

It's great to see Dan again. I haven't seen him for 20 years. In fact, I wouldn't have recognized him if it hadn't been for the suit.

It's touching how Dan and Daisy always hold hands when they are out. If he lets go, she shops.

Like most husbands Dan knows how to say nothing. However, after 28 years he still hasn't learned when to say it.

Sometimes Dan's wheel is spinning but his hamster is asleep.

You only have to be near Dan to lower your IQ.

Senses

When one or more of the five **senses** are incorporated in your speech, they add richness and depth, lifting a speech's potential impact from one-dimensional to multi-dimensional. Senses weaved into a speech add texture, color, and depth in the audience's minds as it changes from flat to full.

The five senses are: **Sight. Hearing. Smell. Taste. Touch.** They are easily remembered by visualizing your face: Eyes. Ears. Nose. Mouth. Chin.

To demonstrate the additive power of evoking sensation, imagine writing a speech about your recent visit to France. Enrich it by drawing on what you experienced through your senses during your first night in Paris. For example, did you: **See** the brightly lit Eiffel Tower? **Hear** the taxis' loud klaxons? **Smell** tempting aromas wafting from cozy little bistros? Delight your palate with your first **taste** of *foie gras*? Allow your hand to run along the balustrade of one of the many Seine bridges, **touching** the same stonework smoothed by millions before you?

An excellent example, where three senses (touch, smell, and sight) created a richer scene, comes from Vikas Jhingran [07]:

One afternoon, Mom and I travelled to the old part of the city of Calcutta, India. Here, the houses were so close that sunlight was a myth. The aroma of spices drifted in the hot humid air. And in a small hut sat the holy man everyone called the Swami. His saffron robe drenched in sweat, he tried to solve the problems put before him.

Of course, you don't have to go to India to create your scenes: you can create a senses-suffused speech just talking about your backyard with all you can touch there, along with its sounds, sights, smells, and tastes.

Following, you will see other examples of how Senses have been used in speeches.

[Woof. Owwwooo.] I was surrounded by a pack of black and tan hunting hounds. [Owwwooo!!] My heart jumped. Then so did I—to the trunk, and then the roof of Fat Dad's new car. Frozen like a treed raccoon, I was screaming and bawling <pause> the hounds were howling and circling. An ugly one-eyed dog clawed and scratched his way onto the trunk, his yellow teeth snapping and foaming. <pause> His claws screeched and slipped on the glass. [04]

I had just spent the day in front of one of the most beautiful structures built by man [the Taj Mahal]. But I couldn't recall the touch of the radiant, white marble or the elaborate carvings on the pillars. I didn't remember the smell of the flowers that surrounded the structure or the details of the spectacular dome. It was almost like I had just seen a—postcard. [07]

The theater is quiet. The aroma of overpriced popcorn permeates the air. [03]

66

What the boy remembered most
About his first visit to the ICU—
Was the smell.
It smelled like somebody threw up
Or somebody's puppy had an accident
And whoever cleaned it
Used buckets and buckets of Pine Sol
To try to hide the smell. [10DH]

Until one day Miss Mamo went "ugh"
[Put his hand to his chest]
And that machine that goes *beep, beep*
Starts going *beep, beep, beep, beep,*
And a nurse rushed in
And a doctor rushed in
And when it seemed like that machine
couldn't *beep* any faster—or Miss Mamo's
face couldn't get any tighter
Something happened …
Miss Mamo relaxed.
She looked peaceful.
And that machine went *beeeep*
[Draws a straight line with hand].
Confused, sad, and scared, our young
doctor melted into a corner. [10DH]

My Grandmother's kitchen was filled with
the aroma of freshly cooked bread, and
the quiet rhythmic chopping of vegetables
was the only sound to be heard. [09]

That unforgettable little girl, whose hair
smelled of strawberry shampoo. [15BT]

The next morning I drove my car to the
service station [to remove a long scratch].
The service station was filled with an
aroma of polish–aaah! [15-2]

Go to the forest of Fontainebleau, France,
in Spring with a desire to have a leisurely
walk. You can't. There is something
about the crispness of the air. There is
something about the smell of the trees.
You want to run. Do something. [SG]

Maybe you know what's it's like to have
to sit at the bedside of a loved one who
is going to die. Her eyes were yellow;
jaundice had set in. [15PH]

When Mama was sitting watching TV,
Fat Dad would come up behind her, wrap
his strong arms around her, rest his chin
on her shoulder, kiss her on the cheek.
[Sound of puckered kiss] [04]

Much of Obama's route through Havana
could be traced with the scent of fresh tar. [N]

Richard Spencer[93-RS] opened by introducing
us to his father who had very strong
convictions on everything. To cover over
his father's frequent cuss words, Richard
held a child's small bicycle bulb horn. He
squeezed it a lot!

The speedboat hit me—and I submerged
into a touchless, tasteless, sightless,
soundless abyss. [16RM]

Angela Louie[05-2] opened with a short
delightful Chinese lullaby related to her
daughter's birth and ended with a similar
soothing lilt. Many other WSC contestants
have also sung a few lines (with equal
enthusiasm and varying rhythm) including
Arabella Bengson[86], Mark Brown[95], Jim
Key[03], Randy Harvey[04], and LaShunda
Rundles[08].

Other speakers have threaded a unique
sound throughout their speeches. Two
notables were Lance Miller[05] with his
repetition of *Chi-chink* (the sound of
validating a parking ticket) and Presiyan
Vasilev[13] with a high-pitched *squeak,
squeak, squeak* the four times he worked
his rusty car jack.

Similes

A simile compares two things using connecting words such as *like, as, so, than*, or various verbs, such as *resemble*.

For example, these are similes:

As irresistible as a free lunch ...
Like the memories that meander in a midnight cigarette ...

Similes are similar to Metaphors but are typically less direct and more poetic in nature. They add interest, color, exaggeration, and even a smile to a speech. Besides, they are a wonderful vehicle to let your mind conjure up all sorts of creative comparisons as the following examples show:

A woman needs a man like a fish needs a bicycle. [GS]

And then, just as you would take a cookie and dip it into a glass of milk, the sun dipped into the ocean and a few moments later it was gone. [99]

As certain as tomorrow's sunrise [RH]

As contagious as measles

As current as tomorrow's headlines

As excited as Robison Crusoe seeing a footprint on the beach

As forgotten as parents

As green as Kermit the Frog

As idle as a painted ship, upon a painted ocean [STC]

As inevitable as grass growing

As phony as a $3 bill

As long ago as when the first caveman burned his finger

As monotonous as a ticking clock

As nervous as a long-tailed cat in a room full or rocking chairs [RH]

As old as the cave paintings of Altamira [NP]

As spineless as a sea full of jellyfish

As unlikely as fur on a fish

As vivid as a nightmare

As wise as Warren Buffet

Avoid retirement as you would poison ivy in a nudist camp.[83]

Cut down like Kansas corn [RH]

Disappears like dew on a hot day

Dressed like a paragon of preppydom

Entering his office was like going into a museum—plenty to admire, nothing to be touched.

Excited as a 3-year old at Christmas

Flitting from place to place like a hummingbird on steroids

Government is as extravagant and top-heavy as a Dr. Seuss castle.

Grinning like a mule eating kudzu

He turned, and a smile came across his face like butter on hot grits. [11AT]

He was as icily remote as Iceland.

He was as polished as my grandmother's silver service.

He was as square as a game of checkers.

He was like Horatio defending the indefensible bridge.

His soothing words run over you like hot fudge syrup.

His tie was as eye-catching as a $7 bill.

I leaned back, as cool as a hockey puck. RM.^

I woke in a hospital with machines lurking over me like vultures: a doctor to my left, a nurse to my right. 10-2

If our aims are large and our means modest then, like a mouse, we must nibble at those grand goals reducing them to their component parts. 94-3

Just like this flower is unique, you are unique. 14

Life is like a garden that flourishes with the hoe of recognition and the fertilizer of praise.

Like a beautiful tapestry hiding a cement wall

Like a frog, I was spending my time just jumping from lily pad to lily pad.

Like a hamster on its treadmill

Like a human bulldozer mom plows through the crowd—"Son, what happened?" 12

Like a long relationship it was an exercise in irritation management.

Like a postage stamp he sticks to one thing till he gets there.

Like Domino's, he always delivers.

Like flute players in an orchestra, they went to work exactly on cue.

Like one of those annoying hotel alarm clocks, it woke me up. 12

Like swimming through peanut butter

Like toothpaste—easy to let out but impossible to put back

My words are like the stars that never change. Whatever Seattle says, the great chief in Washington can rely upon with as much certainty as he can upon the return of the sun or the seasons. CS

Nursing homes are filled with people who cling to their regrets like security blankets. 83

Reading this book was like eating potato chips; I just couldn't stop.

Several years later, while going through my attic, I found those pink beeswax candles—crumbled like crackers for soup. GA.

She looked at me the way my mom looked at my dad after he forgot their anniversary. 10

She was like a Pekinese floating around on a cushion of charisma. RC.

Snuggled tight like Pringles in a can

Stands out like a wart on a bald head

Telephone poles flashed by like a picket fence.

We must make the most of our gifts—otherwise we are as useless as a sundial in the shade. CR

Your life is like a thermostat. You can dial it down or you can dial it up. 15-JJ

Speech Preparation

TED asks its potential speakers a simple question: What is your message and why does it matter?

Experienced Toastmasters suggest we break that down into more detail:

- What is my message or point?
- Why is it important to me? And my audience?
- What do I want them to Think, Feel or Do?
- What can I do to help them remember my message?
- Am I excited by my message? [If not, why should my audience?]

The hardest question for speakers always seems to be: *What should I talk about?* To which the ideal answer is: Something personal that is meaningful to you, accompanied by related supporting stories that you will deliver with emotion.

The best approach I know came from my mentor[RH] who asked:

- **Who** are the 4 most important influences in my life?
- **What** was the most important lesson each taught?
- **Why** do I remember each lesson? (What was the triggering occasion)?

Reviewing those answers, decide which is the most important message that you want to share with this audience. That becomes the core of your speech. Then decide the best speech structure for its delivery.

Two of the simplest structures comprise either one or three stories (or scenes). The former covers one thread of thought, eg, The Day I Discovered the Meaning of Appreciation; the latter breaks the speech into three parts, each reinforcing the message in different ways, eg, Appreciation is as old as history; Appreciation is worldwide; Appreciation is needed by those closest to you.

Summaries follow of successful one- and three-story speeches showing how others have used these two structural approaches:

One story

Aditya Maheswaran[15-2] centered his speech on his latest, greatest love—his new car—with other relationships and lessons learned revolving around it.

David Henderson[10] in *The Aviators* tells how his childhood love for Jackie began at age seven with them as aviators in their make-believe planes, fighting the Red Baron. Their beautiful story keeps unfolding, with him learning life's lessons as Jackie is hit with sickle cell anemia and dies seven years later.

David Sanfacon[03-2] whose title *The Script of Your Life* appropriately covered the vagaries of his life from 5th grade to the present as he dealt with who was writing the script of his life.

Ed Hearn[06] built a whole speech around a punching ball he had as an 8-year old, a metaphor for his message that *Bouncing Back* (the title) is the key to handling life's problems.

Ed Tate[00] in *One of Those Days* kept us engaged as he tells his story of one day in his life that began with a speeding ticket and ended boarding a flight to Phoenix, with lots of ups, downs, and surprises in between.

Patrick Hammond[15-PH] centered his speech on the fatherly but professional relationship he developed with a young girl who had been inveigled into the sex trafficking industry.

Presiyan Vasilev[13] describes how a flat tire changed his thinking about life. The speech covers less than an hour of time as he learns how to handle a flat tire when on a downward-sloping road.

Vikas Jhingran[07VJ] in *Postcard* describes how after visiting the Taj Mahal, where his mind was constantly distracted, it was, to him, like seeing a postcard because he wasn't "in the moment." This made him realize he had been living his life like a postcard—flat and incomplete.

Three stories

At age 70, Roy Fenstermaker[83] gave his winning speech titled, appropriately, *Retirement—Never!* He amusingly elaborated that we do three things: don't quit; keep busy; and don't look back.

In a cleverly opened speech, titled *Que Sera* (Will I be happy? Will I be rich? … the future's not ours to see) Jock Elliott[94-3] went on to imaginatively talk about each of those three issues.

In speeches prior to competing for the WSC title, Ed Hearn[06] used a 3-story structure. In *The Courage to Try*, he addresses the reasons why we don't try: our Feelings of Inadequacy, the Convenience of Excuses, and our Fear of Failure. And in his Semifinal speech, *Tearing Down the Walls That Hinder our Greatness,* he explains how we can overcome the three Walls of Self Doubt, Impossibility, and of Mediocrity.

Jock Elliott[11] in *Just So Lucky* spoke of his three best friends—of his blood, his times, and his heart. To help the audience remember them, he identified a different part of the stage for each and spoke about each from each area.

Ryan Avery[12], in *Trust is a Must*, shows his personal journey dealing with Trust, an important value: at high school he breaks his mother's trust (drinking); then a business partner breaks Ryan's trust; and the third scene has him at the altar, now with understanding, pledging his complete trust to his bride-to-be.

Steve Jobs' famous Stanford Commencement Address began: *I want to tell you three stories from my life…* and he went on to speak of the three different influential elements.

Stuart Pink[12-3] spoke of creativity in his speech, *Brain Lifting*. He exemplified his point with 3 diverse stories involving his young son, a student who wanted to go to Italy, and a slow learner who wanted to learn chess.

The Master of breaking speeches into three stories (or subsets) was John Wesley, the founder of the Methodist Church. He taught his preachers that their sermons should comprise only three sections, ideally with one word to identify each section (to easily alliterate or otherwise memorize). Within each, have three sub-subjects, and within each of them, three more, etc. It's a great way to remember speeches from 3 minutes to 3 hours in length!

Speech Opening

Dana LaMon[92] believes the most important part of a speech is the Opening. Why? Because that's when the audience decides whether it's worth listening any further. Their thinking? —Based on what I'm hearing, do I really care to continue listening to this speaker for the next 6-60 minutes?

What opening attention-grabbing techniques are used to solve this problem? The most common are: ◆ arousing curiosity; ◆ asking a mind-catching question; ◆ making a statement followed up by a question; ◆ telling a story; ◆ making a bold statement; ◆ surprise; ◆ using a prop; ◆ reciting a quotation; ◆ referring to a recent conversation or previous speaker; and ◆ asking the audience to imagine something.

Of the above, two of the easiest and extremely effective opening techniques that immediately engage an audience from your opening word are Curiosity and Questions. Start with them. Examples follow:

Curiosity

Title: *Get Up!* [96]

The wind was blowing through my hair
The adrenalin was pulsating through my young body—
The ecstasy! The excitement!
The rush of air fills my senses—
I was 6 years old—
On a bicycle
For the first time in my life.

Title: *Nuggets of Love* [16SS]

Can a chicken nugget change the world? My first job when I was 16 was at McDonald's—and my career has pretty much gone downhill since then.

Title: *Sticks And Stones Will Break Your Bones, But Words Will Never Hurt You— It's A Lie!* [RH]

Sticks and stones will break your bones, but words will never hurt you. It's a lie!!!! Fellow Toastmasters and guests, nothing could be further from the truth ...

Title: *The Key to Fulfillment* [99]

Years ago
I had many conversations—
With myself.
Some contemplating my life—
But unfortunately
Many were contemplating my death.

Title: *The Aviators* [10]

[The speaker is wearing an earlier-era fighter pilot's garb: soft leather aviator cap, jacket, etc.]
In 1983, the two best pilots in Texas teamed up to fight the Red Baron. We called ourselves the Aviators. [Makes fighter plane noise.] "Snoopy One to Snoopy Two, I see him. Break hard right."

Title: *My Little World* [98]

I was the kind of kid
Your parents told you not to play with.
You probably remember me—
The Detention Hall's only permanent resident.

Title: *The Power of Words* [15]

[Puts cigarette in his mouth, pulls out a lighter, looks around ... laughter] What? All of you all think smoking kills? Let me tell you something. Do you know that the amount of people dying from diabetes is three times the number of people dying from smoking?

Title: *The Swami's Question* [07]

[Holding up an envelope]

My hands were shaking. My throat was dry. In my hand was the letter that could change my life. It was from M.I.T. Would it begin Congratulations!—or—You've got to be kidding?

Question

Title: *We Can Be Pygmalion* [86]

Come with me to Ancient Greece. One sculptor, Pygmalion, loved his statue so much it turned into life …
How many of you know the story? How many of you believe this can happen?

Title: *A Warm Boot* [97]

I want to come out
To the front of the stage
So everyone can get a good look
At this guy. [All smiles]
Last year I got a letter from AARP
Saying I was 50.
You know what I mean, don't you?

Title: *Ouch!* [01]

Can you remember a moment when a brilliant idea flashed into your head? It was perfect for you—then all of a sudden from the depths of your brain another thought forced its way through the enthusiasm until finally it shouted, "YEAH great idea, but what if you—fall on your face?" [Speaker falls on his face on stage]

Title: *Unexpected Journey* [10PH]

What do you do when the Universe buys you a bus ticket, puts you on the bus, and gives you the voice of a bullfrog? [10PH]

Title: *Hey! Watch This!* [DW.]

What is it about a motorcycle
That makes grown men

Throw caution to the wind?
Why is it when we climb aboard
One of those bad boys
We become BAD BOYS?

Title: *Perfect* [VJ]

Let me ask you a question that may seem strange.
How many of you chose your parents?
How many chose your children?—
How many wish you had!

Title: *Quart Size Bag Thinking* [10MD]

In the past three years how many of you have been on a plane?
Then you've experienced the quart-sized bag constraint …You know the constraint—3 oz size fluid containers fitting in a quart size bags.

[This metaphor introduced a speech on the constraints we put on our thinking]

Title: *Brain Lifting* [12-3]

Do you like running? Do you belong to a gym, like fifty million Americans do? Mr Contest Chair, fellow Toastmasters, have you ever had that feeling you're in the wrong place at the wrong time?

Title: *Four Words* [14-2]

Have you ever met somebody who just drove you nuts? Yeah—all the married couples are nodding their heads. But more often than not, it's the people closest to us—our friends, our families, our loved ones. They're the ones who frustrate us the most.

Title: *A Gift From Grammie* [15EF]

Without exception—we all have that one special birthday. Can you remember yours? For some, it's sweet sixteen; others, the day that we can drink–legally; and, for others …

Speech Closing

Most speakers seek to deliver a memorable message. In other words, to persuade our listeners to Think, Feel, or Do (TFD) something differently as a result of hearing what we say.

Your whole speech must be crafted with that in mind, and as you close, it's important to remind your audience *why* they should Think, Feel or Do something specific. As in the commercial world, the closing may be a "hard sell" ("Do this...") or it may be a more indirect "soft sell". Your message and the nature of your audience will help you decide which is more appropriate.

One popular way of closing a speech is with a callback to the title. This ties the whole speech together by connecting the ending to the beginning. For new speakers, it's an excellent starting point as it's easy, comfortable, and safe.

Following are examples of Closings using this Callback to Title technique, together with a sampling of other closing methods for your later speeches.

Closing With a Callback to Title

Title: *A Second Chance*

And the fantasy
Will never become reality
Unless we attack the beast
The real beast
Intolerance, indifference and ignorance
Yes—let's kill the beast.
Because everyone
Deserves a second chance.[95]

Title: *Being Jane*

If we accept the past
Be flexible with the future
Then we can live the present
There is so much to gain—
By being Jane [10-3]

Title: *Bloody But Unbowed*

Whatever the outcome, you'll be able to
    stand erect proudly and declare—
"Under the bludgeoning of chance,
My head is bloody but unbowed." [95-2]
[The title is a key line in *Invictus*,
    Henley's poem on courage.]

Title: *Bouncing Back*

What really matters most in life is when we get punched or tilted over or even knocked to the ground—we have to ask ourselves what are we going to do about it? And—more importantly—what is our strategy for Bouncing Back? [06]

Title: *Finding the Right Shoes*

At times, we always think it's about finding the right shoes. But in actual fact, it's about fitting into the shoes that are destined for you. Have you ever thought about that? My shoes, they fit me just right. I have no regrets. Now, I ask you. Do your shoes fit right—or do you still want to trade? [12-2]

Title: *Music In The Key Of Life*

Music might not save the world
But it eases the toils and strife
Because music is written
In the key of life. [02]

Title: *Scratch*

Friends, sometimes in life we are scratched and sometimes we scratch. But, hey, that's life. Scratches are inevitable, but remember, a scratch stays only as long as we don't polish it [out][15-2]

Title: *We Can Fix It*

My friends, if you have any problem, in any relationship, try to pull less and bend more. If you do, I'm sure, we can... [Audience response] "Fix it!" [15-3]

Title: *The Ride of Life*

And will you succeed?
Yes, you will indeed—
"98 and 3/4 percent guaranteed!"—
If you get back on the ride. [04-3]

Title: *The Script of Your Life*

Your Act 1 and your Act 2 may be over. Act 3 begins when you walk out of these doors today. Are you ready?
The Script of Your Life—
Act 3—Scene 1—Action! [03-2]

Other Closing Examples
Soft Closings

The fight against such misconceptions
Can never be won by fist—
Or force of arms.
It is a victory that can only be won
In the hearts and minds
Of each one of us.[79-3]

Friends, have you ever looked inside?—
What if the answer to your problems is not outside?
What the Swami asked me then,
I ask you now—
"Who are you"? [07]

Surprise Closings

I want to leave you with one thing. This one thing is more powerful than anything I could ever say as a speaker. More meaningful than anything I can ever say as a Toastmaster. I want to leave you with this... [Speaker is then silent for 12 seconds] ... Madam Contest Master [99]

Oh! And one more thing—you've been a wonderful audience! [05]

Invitational Closings

My invitation to you is this ... [TR]

Fellow Toastmasters,
Hope is the best medicine
So if you have lost touch with someone who needs it
Then write them a prescription
Before it is too late. [10DH]

Give your audience the option to accept your idea either now or when the time is right, eg, the next time you find a nickel in your hand then ...

Tonight, remember that you can make a difference. The question you must ask yourself is 'How?' ...

Toastmasters
Let me challenge you to take control
And give out words of life
To encourage those
That you touch every day.
It's an investment you can make—
Without spending a dime.
It's interest you can draw—
Freely given.
You have the power.
Go forward.
Give life. [04RH]

Poetic Closings

I don't know what life has to offer next
And it may be way out of line
But there is no reason to fret & whine
For though you didn't cause your sorry plight
You do have the power to make it right
After all, everything in life is arranged—
until you make it perfect. [VJ]

Surprise

Surprises are when over-sized "non-expectations" occur, usually as Twists, unanticipated "Firsts," or misdirections on a mind-grabbing scale.

Probably the best-known Toastmasters Surprise was Darren LaCroix[01] falling flat on his face 20 seconds into his speech and then speaking to the Toastmaster and the audience for a short period from there.

An earlier, equally creative, Surprise occurred at a 1974 Toastmasters Regional Contest. Picture this: The speaker walks onto the stage wiping his brow. Head down, with a shaky voice, he says: "After hearing the previous three speakers, I realize I am not good enough to compete. I'm sorry if I've caused any problems but I won't be able to give my speech." Then he sits down—in front of a shocked audience. The Contest Chair walks to the lectern where, with a quizzical look, says: "Well, I guess, on with the show ..." But before the next contestant could be announced, the speaker leaps from his chair, shouting, "Please sit down!" Turning to a puzzled but now fascinated audience he asks, "How many times do we see people ready to quit before they even start—just like that previous speaker who was ready to give up? How often does the fear of failure prevent us from doing things we really can do?" This truly dramatic Surprise opening helped Joel Weldon earn top honors enabling him to compete at the WCPS where he placed third.

Now, a Surprise doesn't have to be so dramatic. It can be created with everyday items, even shoes. Palaniappa Subramaniam[12-2] walked onto the stage wearing a white gym shoe and a black formal shoe (another unexpected First!) saying he couldn't decide what to wear so he read the contest dress code and found it was semi-formal. "So I came prepared!"

Bill Gove, a great speaker, surprised in this way: "I used to play golf each Tuesday with a group of Oldies. [Turns to surprised audience] You are supposed to shout out there: *How old were they?*" [Starts over] "I used to play golf each Tuesday with a group of Oldies." [Audience shouts out]: *How old were they?* [Answers] "Well, I'm glad you asked that question..."

The following "non-expectations" provide more ideas for you:

Title: *I Fell In Love With A Prostitute*

How do you react to a title like that? The speaker began by asking leading questions to an imaginary person—we wondered, *Where is this going?*—and were surprised to learn that she was a child, a 3-year "veteran" of the LA child sex-trafficking trade. [15-PH]

Title: *Que Sera*

When I was just a little boy
I asked my mother:
What will I be?
Will I be handsome?
Will I be rich?
Here's what she said to me.
She said—No! [94-3]

Bill Gates, during his 2009 TED speech on eradicating malaria, opened a jar of mosquitos and let them fly freely into the room to a very surprised (and anxious) audience.

Examining his life, the speaker[LM] had realized that one of his great strengths was paying his bills on time. Later, when wondering what his tombstone should read, his mind answered him: "759"—his credit card score!

Rory Vaden[07-2] surprised us with a speaking "No-No" by opening—and closing—his speech with his back to the audience.

Speaker can offer a surprising statistic such as: There are 18,000 books on the Internet about success and 452,000 websites for motivational speakers. They all have a magical formula for our success! [06RH] [Here's another surprising statistic to ask: How many years are one trillion seconds? Answer: 31,700]

Oh, there's one more thing—was a phrase Steve Jobs sometimes added at the apparent end of a presentation, but went on to surprise his audience by announcing a new feature or product.

Ask the audience a question they should know the answer to, but often don't, eg, "Quick—what building is on most nickels?" [Use if starting a speech on, say, Monticello or Jefferson.]

My thesis was due in 3 months.
I procrastinated and procrastinated.
Did nothing until the last 3 days—
Worked non-stop 72 hours.
Sprinted it across Campus.
Just met the deadline. Phew!
One week later—phone call.
The School.
"Tim Urban?"
Yeah.

"We need to talk about your thesis."
Okay.
"It's the best one we've seen!"
[Big pause.]
That did not happen!!!
It was a bad paper—I just wanted to enjoy that moment when you thought this guy was amazing! [Laughter]
[Synopsis of part of TED Speech, Feb 2016, by Tim Urban, that provided suspense and a fun double Surprise.]

Misdirection

You can misdirect the audience by making a statement that gets heads nodding in agreement and then surprise them by disagreeing. For example, Zig Ziglar asked one audience to complete: *Anything worth doing is—[worth doing well]*. Flipping, he then convinced them: *Anything is worth doing poorly—until you can do it well.*

Do you know what is wrong with the world? Do you know what is wrong with me? Do you know what is wrong with you?—WHO CARES!!??? [05]

Ready! Aim!—Blame! [00-MH]

Word Surprises

I'd do it, <u>but</u> I'm too old.
I'd do it, <u>but</u> I'm not smart enough.
I'd do it, <u>but</u> I never have time.
But . . . But . . . But ...
If don't get off our butts
We'll be frozen to that bucket [94]

I'm <u>too</u> busy; I'm <u>too</u> afraid; I'm <u>too</u> involved ... Friends—take off your excuse "<u>tutu</u>" [As the speaker[07-BP] pantomimed stepping out of a tutu]

Titles

Your title is not trivial. It is your opportunity to entice the audience to "sit up and listen up" for what's to follow. It opens your speech without you even saying a word. The ideal title engages the audience's mind and starts them thinking—grabbing their attention without giving away too much.

Two excellent examples are Earl Nightingale's classic, *The Strangest Secret,* and Morgan McArthur's *Boredom Insurance: Don't work another day without it.* Both capture our curiosity and increase our anticipation.

Aspirational and inspirational speeches are known for their attention-arousing titles. Two favorite examples are *Turn Your Scars Into Stars*[RS] and *Don't Settle for Greatness When You Can Be Immortal.*[04RH] Many speakers let their titles do double duty, acting both as a curiosity-arouser and as a memory hook for the speech. Examples of such include: *I See Something in You,*[14] *We Can Fix It,*[15-3] *Always Take an Empty Suitcase,* and *Our Quietest Freedom.*

Titles may have a different "feel" depending on the type of speech (Informational vs. Inspirational vs. Entertaining). For example, 18-minute TED presentations are often more informational in nature whereas the content of 7-minute Toastmaster Speech Contests are typically more Inspirational or Entertaining.

It's fun reading speech titles—we wonder what words actually followed and what we would talk about if using those titles.

As you review the following actual speech titles, decide which appeal to you most. Ask yourself why? Use that insight as you plan your own.

TED's 20 Most Popular Speeches

Do Schools Kill Creativity?
Your Body Language Shapes Who You Are
How Great Leaders Inspire Action
 The Power Of Vulnerability
My Stroke Of Insight
The Thrilling Potential Of SixthSense
    Technology
10 Things You Didn't Know About Orgasm
Why We Do What We Do
The Puzzle Of Motivation

Underwater Astonishments
The Surprising Science Of Happiness
The Power Of Introverts
Meet The SixthSense Interaction
Your Elusive Creative Genius
The Best Stats You've Ever Seen
How To Spot A Liar
The Happy Secret To Better Work
How I Held My Breath For 17 Minutes
Brain Magic
Looks Aren't Everything. Believe Me,
    I'm A Model

Some WCPS Titles

Retirement? Never! [83]
We Can Be Pygmalion [86]
The Pain Passes [87]
Please Don't Walk on Mother's Roses[88]
A Many-Splendored Thing [89]
Silver Bullets [90]
The Train's Still Rollin' [91]
Take A Chance [92]
It's Possible [93]
Stuck to a Bucket [94]
A Second Chance [95]
Get Up! [96]
A Warm Boot [97]
My Little World [98]
The Key to Fulfillment [99]
One of Those Days [00]
Ouch! [01]
Music in the Key of Life [02]
Never Too Late [03]
Fat Dad [04]
The Ultimate Question [05]
Bouncing Back [06]
The Swami's Question [07]
Speak [08]
A Sink Full of Green Tomatoes [09]
The Aviators [10]
Just So Lucky [11]
Trust is a Must [12]
Changed by a Tire [13]
I See Something in You [14]
The Power of Words [15]
Outsmart; Outlast [16]

Other Interesting Titles

A Gift From Grammie [15EF]
A Precious Gift [11-KB]
Afraid of the Dog [12-KRM]
Alice in Blunderland
Being Jane [10-3]
Big Red Balloon [10KYY]

Bless! Not Impress! [09-MZ]
Bloodied But Unbowed [95-2]
Brain Lifting [12-3]
Buried Treasures [96-2]
Catch the Right Bus
Celebrate the Common Man
Crazy [02-3]
Does It Matter?
Dorothy Was Right [LM]
Expectations
Finding the Right Shoes [12-2]
Four Words [14-2]
Goodbye WI-FI [14-3]
Inspirate—Don't Motivate [RM.]
It's Time [BM]
Knockout [79-3]
Life Is A Marathon
Look for the Open Window [98-3]
My Alter Ego [10-2]
No Doubt [01-2]
Nothing Better Than [13-JW]
On the Sideline [10RG]
Ordinary People
Plain Jane [10-3]
Que Sera [94-3]
Rematch! [10LC]
Scratch [15-2]
Some Words are Diamonds [94-2]
The Best Medicine [10DH]
The Box [11-OR]
The Difference is Horsepower [93-2]
The Greatest Gift
The Journey [97-2]
The Ride of Life [04-3]
The Script of Your Life [03-2]
The Sitting Place [13-2]
The Spirit Within [05-2]
To Be A Legend
Underneath [99-2]
Unexpected Journey [10PH]
We Can Fix It [15-3]
Yet Here I Stand [12-DP]

Triples

From Aristotle's *Ethos, Pathos, and Logos*; Julius Caesar's *Veni, Vidi, Veci*; and the Bible's account of *Three Wise Men* carrying gifts of *gold, frankincense, and myrrh* right down through history to today's expressions of *The Good, the Bad, and the Ugly;* a morning cereal that goes *Snap, Crackle, Pop;* and, *It's a bird. It's a plane. It's Superman!* we see words and phrases in sets of three. **Triples** (or Triads or Trios) have played a key role in our spoken and written language throughout history.

Why? Because Triples give a feel of balance and completeness, offer a pleasant rhyming sound, and enable easy memorization, making them one of the most frequently used tools in every speaker's toolbox.

The following examples offer a general overview that will start snapping your synapses into action. Triples are easy to create, deliver, and understand, and they combine well with many other tools such as Alliteration, Repetition, and Twists. It's likely that every speech you give from now on will have at least one Triple tucked inside. Always remember, words in threes please.

General Examples

Emile Griffith, tall, slender, quietly spoken. [79-3]

I'm sorry to be so wishy-washy—but I am absolutely, unequivocally, and decidedly unsure.

My great grandfather never grew rich, or tall, or old. [06-JE]

My precious daughter wanted the Barney Song ... so with <u>quivering voice</u>, <u>trembling lips</u>, and <u>breaking heart</u> ... she sang. [01-2]

Ninety-year old Ida expressed how overwhelmed she was by the overflowing church, the heartfelt eulogies, the mountain of letters. [03-BW]

She had been my inspiration, my focus, my lighthouse in stormy seas. [95-2]

Some books should be tasted, some devoured, but only a few should be chewed and digested thoroughly. [FB]

The best doctor in the whole wide world does more than stitch up cuts, push pills, or take out tonsils—he gives people hope. [10DH]

We have killed each other with our ignorance, our prejudice, and our silence. [MF]

Within 6 months we grew apart. There was no holding of hands, no music, no yoga. [15-3]

Enriched with Alliteration

Don't wait until it's too late to <u>l</u>ive, to <u>l</u>earn, and to <u>l</u>ove. [15EF]

A victim of the real beast—intolerance, indifference, and ignorance [95]

There are three ways to handle a situation that might arouse anger: alter it, avoid it, or adapt to it. [02DS]

With a change in direction

Think of Plato—with his radical idealism, intellectual rigidity, and hatred of the mob. [SL^]

We pledge our best efforts to help them ... not because the Communists may be doing it, not because we seek their votes, but because it is right. [JFK]

One triple following another

In <u>20 campaigns</u>, on <u>100 battlefields</u>, around <u>1,000 camp fires</u>, I have witnessed that <u>enduring fortitude</u>, that <u>patriotic self-abnegation</u>, and that <u>invincible determination</u> which have carved his statue in the hearts of his people. [DM]

We do not propose to petition the legislature to make our husbands <u>just, generous, and courteous</u> ... we think it in violation of every principle of <u>taste, beauty, and dignity</u> [ECS]

We hold these truths to be <u>self-evident</u>, that all men are created <u>equal</u>, that they are endowed by their Creator with certain <u>unalienable Rights</u>, that among these are <u>Life, Liberty and the pursuit of Happiness</u> [DOI]

Without books ... history is silent, science is crippled, thought and speculation is at a standstill ... They are the windows of the world, the engines of change, the lighthouses in the sea of time [BT+]

Revolving around one idea

Our hometown, where we learned ... such values as honor, integrity, and self-respect [90]

Mama treated me to a hickory stick waltz. You know what I mean—A piece of kindling taken from the wood box applied to the backside in steady rhythms. You sing along in <u>keys, chords, and crescendos</u>. [04RH]

When you feel overwhelmed, under-appreciated and utterly alone; when you have fallen, failed, and been forgotten, you can still achieve greatness if you resolve to do the work. [16EE] [Double]

Triples that Rhyme

Aspire to inspire before you expire!

I dream of a home that is spacious, gracious, and palacious. [MVH]

Homeless, useless, worthless [95]

Triples that follow a sequence

And gradually bit by bit, step by step, day by day, we will achieve ... [94-3]

Been there. Done that. Got the T-Shirt[11]

Change is the law of life. Those who look only to the past or present are certain to miss the future [JFK]

Civilization begins with order, grows with liberty, and dies with chaos. [WD+]

Even though Grammie had lost her home, lost her husband, and lost her hearing, she wasn't just surviving her spirit was thriving. [15EF]

Every great cause begins as a movement, becomes a business, and eventually degenerates into a racket. [EH]

Sixty years—60 months—60 minutes. What is time?

We meet at a <u>college</u> noted for knowledge, in a <u>city</u> noted for progress, in a <u>State</u> noted for strength, and we stand in need of all three, for we meet in an <u>hour</u> of change and challenge, in a <u>decade</u> of hope and fear, in an <u>age</u> of both knowledge and ignorance.[JFK] [Double Triple Sequence]

We started to plan a reunion. But, as it usually does, life got in the way, and our reunion went from a definite day—to some day—to one day. [15EF]

Socrates taught Plato. Plato taught Aristotle. Aristotle taught Alexander the Great—who conquered the world.

Twists

Gentlemen, you have no idea of the power of a love letter—until your wife intercepts it! [01-3]

The above is the classic **Twist**. J.A. Gamache had us moving in one direction and then—Bam!—completely redirected—we arrived somewhere else! Amidst laughter!

The structure of a Twist is: Short statement—Pause—Surprise redirection.

Most twists are humorous but they can also be serious. They delight your audience and make them think. Not only do they often trigger laughter but they also act as a small mental speed bump recapturing any wandering minds in the audience.

Twists are easy to create. One way is to take any well-known expression and change its expected ending. For example, consider the proverb: *A fool and his money [pause] are soon parted.* By changing the phrase after the pause (ie, the expectation) you create a Twist, as in: *A fool and his money—are invited places*!

A Twist can occur after any number of phrases. Injecting a Twist after a single phrase is most common. In the Humor tool, you will see that a Twist that follows two phrases (the third phrase being the Twist) is the standard formula for humorists. As you read below, you'll discover the diversity and delight of Twists.

A lot of people are afraid of heights. Not me—I'm afraid of widths.

A pessimist is an optimist—but with experience.

A politician is a fellow who will lay down your life for his country. [TG]

Always remember you're unique—just like everyone else. [LM^]

As a candidate, it means open season on his weight, his wit, and his son's arrest record.

Blood is thicker than water—and no one is thicker than my brother. [11]

Eat right, exercise—then die like the rest of us!

Europe's cathedrals: so inspired, so magnificent—so empty [MR]

Give a man a fish and he will eat for a day. Teach him how to fish, and he will sit in a boat and drink beer all day.

Give me your tired, your poor, your fingerprints (describing a political opponent's program).

He was six foot—from shoulder to shoulder.

How many of you know that if you had your life to live over again, you'd do more? How many of you know people who are not living up to their full potential? And how many of you saw one of those people when you looked in the mirror this morning? [10DP]

I had a job I didn't like. I hadn't had a date in three years. And I had a couple of roommates named Mom and Dad. [05]

I promise to tell the truth, the whole truth, and nothing but the truth—unless I think it really adds to my story! [RM.^]

I wanted to give up. The mortgage was due; two car notes were due; and my Toastmaster fees were due. [04-3]

I was walking down the street wearing glasses when the prescription ran out. [SW]

I woke up in the hospital with some memory loss. Doctors examined my brain; they found nothing—nothing wrong with my memory. [10JA]

I'm going to make a prediction—the game could go either way!

I've had a lot of luck over the past three years—all of it bad. [RE]

If you keep doing what you have been doing, you keep on getting <P> less. [LB]

If you need a title, be imaginative. I know an auto mechanic who is now a "vehicle maintenance engineer." He repairs my Toyota—and drives a Mercedes! [83]

If you think health care is expensive now—wait until you see what it costs when it's free. [PO]

In the late 90's, both neophytes and the greedy bought dotcoms with no earnings, no business plan and no clue.

It's the same sort of mentality of those who book their graves in advance—they don't want to miss out on a good spot! [98]

My dad came up to me and said, "Son, it's okay. You've flunked your exams; you already got arrested. That's fine—you get that from your mother's side" [14]

My education was dismal. I went to a series of schools for mentally disturbed teachers. [WA]

My parents worked out that I wasn't a General Manager—I was just being generally managed. [14-2]

My plane left at 5.25—and I didn't.

My popularity shot up—like Apple stock! [07]

My wife and I signed up for ballroom dancing—actually, my wife signed us up for ballroom dancing. [10JG]

The human mind is the most remarkable of all creations. It starts working even before we are born, and works continuously 24 hours a day collecting and storing information, and never stops...until we stand up to give a speech at Toastmasters. [87]

There are three rules of speaking: To be seen one must stand up; to be heard one must speak up; to be appreciated one must sit down. There are three types of lies: lies, damned lies, and statistics. [BD]

There was no way that I was going to stand in some soup line—I don't even like soup. [04-3]

There we were, three macho teenagers, Taylor, Eric and, well—two macho teenagers—and me. [12]

Veni, Vidi, Visa: I came, I saw, I did a little shopping.

We could have been angry at each other or at the GPS [for being in the wrong place]—but instead we chose to be in the present, admiring the beautiful scenery of the wrong hills. [10-3]

You and I are told we must choose between a left or right, but I suggest there is no such thing as a left or right. There is only an up or down. [RR]

You settle in for the perfect family outing, and then it happens: the film you are watching takes a sudden emotional turn. You try to resist, but you can't help it! Before you know it, your eyes begin to—sweat. [03]

Vary Your Visual Speaking Height (VSH)

Man has a primitive reptilian brain. Its function is to help us cope and survive. When variations from the normal occur, it automatically alerts us by instinctively triggering a danger-avoiding response. For example, if a red ball is thrown in front of our car, we swerve or brake as we instinctively respond to avoid hitting a child who may be chasing that ball and/or avoid damage to ourselves or our car.

This also applies to speaking. When a speaker quickly changes from his normal speaking height his reptilian brain automatically goes on alert because something is different from the normal. Therefore, speakers can heighten their audience's awareness level when they vary their visual (normal) speaking height. (*What's going on here?* being an audience member's instinctive reptilian reaction.)

Done sparingly, varying our VSH is a simple way to increase our audience's attention and strengthen our connection with them. It adds valuable visual variety to our speeches for, just as on a journey, hills and valleys beat the monotony of plains.

Two of the easiest ways to begin experimenting with varying your Visual Speaking Height is by sitting on or standing on a chair during part(s) of your speech. Let the following suggest ways to alert the reptilian brains in your audiences:

Chair

Jim Key [03] used two chairs, twice—at the start of his speech when he sprawled out on them at the movies; then, at speech's end, he stands on them imitating a deaf mute girl signing to the audience.[03]

Randy Harvey [04] used a single chair four times, seamlessly, in 7 minutes. He climbs on it (car hood) to escape snarling dogs; He sits on it (driver's seat—and crashes the car); He sits on it (a rock) as his dad comforts him; and a scene has his mother sitting on it while his dad smooches her from behind.

My father-in-law, Frank, and I were sitting [sit on chair] chatting about his business. Something he said surprised me—*People who buy the biggest monuments are often those who have spent least time with the deceased.* [BW.]

Speaker sits on a chair and, later, holds it in one hand above his head using it as an umbrella! [15EB]

Speaker opens by standing on a chair and taking a photo of the audience.

[Speaker sits in chair and faces left] Mr Toastmaster and Guests—Without distinguishing features, every one of you can be reduced to a silhouette. [15KM]

Using the up-ended <u>chair</u> as a metaphor for his deceased Grandpapa's body, the Speaker kneels and softly touches one leg's tip (Grandpapa's toe) as he gives his moving goodbye [01-3]

Falling then Talking from Floor

[After <u>falling face down</u> onto the stage, Speaker continues his audience dialog:] What do you do when you fall on your face? Do you try to jump right up and hope no one noticed? [01]

Speaker jumps out of a crashing plane, falls flat on his face, then starts crawling across stage muttering he refuses to die, refuses to die, because he still has goals to reach [15EB]

Kneeling

Zig Ziglar often came to stage front, knelt on one knee, and talked to that front audience section. Other times he would bend over and then kneel on one knee as he primed his pump [a prop]. And on still other occasions he'd kneel on both knees and talk to us.

Speakers have knelt down to:
Plant seeds [15-GM]
Pick up letters [06-MA]
Pick glass up after an accident [06-RV]

[Kneeling on both knees] ... I implore you—or do I have to beg you? [MA^]

A day may come that make us drop on our knees [drops to knees], a day when we feel we can't even get out of bed. [15EB]

After recounting his litany of problems, the Speaker drops to his knees in worry and then, wondering how and where it all went wrong, he drops his head to the floor in despair. [10-3]

Drop Down to Children's Level

As a small boy [Speaker crouches down] my imagination would take me to the most amazing places [98]

Jana Barnhill leaned over and hugged a child, then got down with him, and, with arms out, scooped up another. And she even played with his blocks. [96-2]

Julia Esguerra knelt to teach a hearing impaired boy to speak—and how to blow his nose! [99-JE]

A week later I walked into his room. And again he is going at it, and this time he was even looking at me. I came down [knelt down] and said, "Sweetie, come here: don't do that—you're a big boy now." [15]

Lean Over

The doctor arrived early one evening to find her but 24 hours from death. He took the husband aside and gently told him the sad news. The burly coalminer groaned. He staggered, stumbled, and dropped down [Speaker acting out the words] by his wife's bed. Grabbing her hands, he cried: "Oh, Edith, Edith, don't go—I need you." [03BW]

Speaker moved a few steps forward (and leaned forward) heightening audience's anticipation. [12]

Speaker, hands above both knees, talks leaning into audience. [06-TL]

Sshhh! Come close. [Speaker leans forward and pulls his audience forward.] I have I something special to tell you. [MMc]

Other VHS Changes

Shurooq AlBanna, statuesque and dressed fully in black, described how her ancestors were pearl divers and then, tilting her head downwards, gracefully put her hands together and imitated the sea dive of her forebears. [13-3]

Speaker enthusiastically runs onto stage, tells of Susie, his teenage Summer-love, and springs up a 10-foot stepladder to her window. [98-3]

Visual Words

Visual words bring your speech to life. They inject energy and project vitality. They are often active verbs, vivid nouns, and colorful adjectives. They include action-oriented words and those that conjure up the senses (smell, sound, etc). They are more likely to be specifics than generalities.

In his book *Emote*, Vikas Jhingran describes research showing that when words create images, our understanding and retention increases. For example, take a commonly used bland word: *walk*. Consider visual words with a similar meaning and his point becomes clear—sashayed, sauntered, scampered, shuffled, skedaddled, skipped, slinked, slouched, sprinted, staggered, strode, strolled, stumbled. And that's just from one letter of the alphabet.

How would you describe what happens when love ends? View this vivid picture projected with visual words by Jock Elliot[11]:

This friendship of lovers can last for the rest of our lives. Or it may burn with the power of a sunburst, hot and bright and brief, to fade and die, leaving two burnt husks, bitter and twisted and scarred.

Visual words often create vivid vignettes that, in turn, create vibrant memories. Breathe vitality and life into your speeches!

From *Perfect* VJ

[A speech on his arranged marriage]

Friends, a few weeks into my marriage
I had been poisoned ...
Poisoned by the "what if" question—
And this doubt and regret
Started to choke the very meaning out of
     my life—
Because—you see—instead
Of strengthening my new marriage
I was already regretting it ...
Until one day I was watching TV
And some crazy guy came on and said
"Everything in life is arranged ... "
And I jumped up and said
"You better believe it."
Now, wait a minute, friends,
Don't tell me
You don't argue with your TV.
You know what the best part is?
You always win
Because if you are losing

You can shut if off and walk away—
Then this crazy man carried on
"Everything in life is arranged—
Until you make it perfect."
"What do you mean?" I shouted...

From *Fat Dad* 04

The car swerved to the left—
Then catapulted right.
Cut down the Morrison's fence—
Sailing through their yard—
Aimed straight at Mossburger's fountain
Where Mary Poppins stood—
Holding her umbrella—
Pouring water from a can.
I hit that fountain so hard
I launched her like Sputnik—
Mary Poppins hovered briefly over the
river <pause>
Then went down faster than a spoonful of
sugar! <pause>
The Morrisons and the Mossburgers were
a bit excited—

Not Fat Dad.
He rode in like the Cavalry
And made peace with the neighbors.[04]

From *A Second Chance* [95]

But Gaston fuels their fear of the
unknown and whips them into a frenzy.
This angry mob cuts down trees, and
they make clubs, they brandish knives,
pitchforks and torches, and they march
through the forest singing, "We don't like
what we don't understand ..."

From *The Script of Your Life* [03-2]

At the age of 20 I found such a script.
It was called "The Art of the Deal."
An autobiography of Donald Trump.
Bye-bye bee keeping. Hello buildings.
Hello Towers. Hello Manhattan. Viva
Las Vegas. Greed is good. Masters of
the Universe. So I shed my beekeeper's
uniform for a suit and tie and I went to
college and majored in economics. I was
on my way [Marches across stage]

From *Knockout* [79-3]

"Seven, Eight, Nine, Out!
The winner
By a knockout in the 12th round
And the new Welterweight Champion
Of the world—Emile Griffith!"
The vast arena erupts in pandemonium
Handlers, admirers, reporters—
Surge forward to sweep the victor off his
feet in triumph.
Against the ropes on the other side
The loser lies in a crumpled heap.
A doctor is summoned. Brain damage!
Emergency surgery! Immediately!
For 10 days Paret lingers in a coma
... and quietly dies.
The fists that struck the fatal blows
Were those of Emile Griffith—
Hooks, upper-cuts, rips had reigned
relentlessly on Paret—the perfect image

of the ring gladiator—slain by a man the
exact opposite.
Tall, slender, quietly spoken—
With the reputation of a gentleman.
But Emile Griffith was more than that.
He designed and made ladies' hats.
And in that simple act—
We find the key to Paret's death.
At the weigh-in before the fight
Paret repeatedly taunted Griffith—
Maricón, faggot, queer—
Making it contemptuously clear
That anyone who made women's hats
Must lack the qualities of manhood
To entitle him to wear the Crown.

From *Ouch!* [01]

Can you remember a moment when a
brilliant idea flashed into your head?—
It was perfect for you—then all of a
sudden from the depths of your brain
another thought forced its way through
the enthusiasm until finally it shouted:
"YEAH great idea, but what if you—fall
on your face?"

From *Some Words Are Diamonds, Some Words Are Stones!* [94-2]

"Do you realize that I almost quit
my musical career because I was so
depressed?" And then she took out a
pen and wrote on a piece of paper [those
words I had told her five years ago] "You
play like a double amputee." She tore it
up in front of me and she said, "And now,
what would you like to eat these with?"

From An Audience of One [16-KH]

In my living room I have a chess set that
my parents brought me from Greece. And
each piece is depicted by a different Greek
mythological god or goddess. I have this
set proudly displayed on a chess table
that my grandmother refinished herself—
over 50 years go.

Vive la différence

When a business launches a new product chances for success are best if the product is First, Different, or Better. Because if it's the same, who will notice it? The same criteria apply when crafting a speech you want to have impact.

Darren LaCroix, WCPS[01], tells those preparing for a speech contest: plan to deliver an 11, on a scale of 1-10! (An "11" is something exceptional ... ideally, something that's never been done before.) His point? Give your audience something memorable, something special to remember you and your message—don't just hope they will.

In *Resonate*, author Nancy Duarte describes an easy-to-remember way to do this: include a STAR moment in your speech. STAR is her acronym for Something They'll Always Remember.

Marketing expresses the logic this way: *Differentiate or die* because *if we don't differentiate, we are invisible.* In speaking, as in marketing, there are three ways to accomplish this: be First, Different, or Better.

The examples below are sorted in these three classifications. What is First and Different is self-defined. Being Better means taking, say, any of the tools in your toolbox and executing them exceptionally well. For example, if you have a beautiful voice, singing some lines appropriate to your speech may add richness to it.

The selection ranges from simple to remarkable, but all are memorable. Let them squeeze your do-something-different juices.

Being First

Albert Mensah[99-2] was the first to wear formalwear of a non-Western culture. With a powerful message that we're all the same underneath, he wor a formal, full-length, multi-color Dinka from his Ghanaian homeland and later removed it to show a Western suit.

Brett Rutledge[98] brought us into the Space Age by engaging in an imaginary laser sword fight with Darth Vader.

Craig Valentine[99] carried on a remarkable two-way dialog with his mirrored reflection.

Douglas Wilson[06-2] opened by standing on back-to-back chairs "sawing" a tree limb, then slipped and fell, cleverly locking his legs into the chairs and addressed the Toastmaster upside down!

Jim Key[03] captured us by ending his speech not with words, but sign language. We understood him because a minute earlier he had signed the same message while vocalizing it.

Michael Aun[78] ran onto stage and then spoke from in front of the lectern.

Mohammed Qahtani[15] opened by putting a cigarette in his mouth, pulling out a lighter, then looked up as the audience collectively anxiously reacted. It was an impactful lead into his speech *The Power of Words.*

Rory Vaden[07-2] opened and closed his speech with his back to the audience! This speaking No-No was an integral and very effective part of the speech.

Being Different

A speaker I've never forgotten drew out 23 feet of tape from his tape measure to demonstrate the length of a Blue Whale at birth—and left it on the floor during the whole speech. [KC.]

Burn victim and paraplegic W Mitchell sometimes opens a speech from his wheelchair just by raising one eyebrow.

Choosing alternative words can add a difference to a speaker, eg, replace "in one week" with either "in 168 hours" or "in 10,080 minutes."

Have an imaginary conversation, not with another person, but with, say, your mind, a mirror, your past or future, a tree, a book or a …

Imagine a speaker who becomes quiet, leans towards the audience while saying "Sssssh!" with a finger on his lips. Then, softly, "Lean close—let me tell you something special." When Morgan McArthur did that we all leaned forward waiting in anticipation for what was to come next …

In his 2009 TED Talk about ending malaria as a big killer, Bill Gates grabbed attention by opening a jar of mosquitos and letting them loose!

Simon Scriver[16SS] differentiated his point cleverly by converting a common 3-word statement into 7 words with big pauses in between—We like to quote Mother Teresa and Martin Luther King and Steve Jobs. We talk about these grand speeches that are going to Change . . . Change . . . Change … the … World . . . World . . . World.

Steve Jobs from time to time would end a speech with "Oh, just one more thing" and go on to announce a new product or feature.

What about an outrageous or absurdly long speech title? Andy Dooley's winning Humorous Speech Contest title was 31 words long! Its title—*A Short But Unbelievably Intriguing Tale Of How Destiny Unexpectedly Showed Her True Colors Against The Backdrop Of Pure White Snow On A Colorado Mountaintop While All Other Conditions Remained Normal.* Think that speech was differentiated before the speaker uttered his first word?

Ten years later, in the 2016 WCPS, Aaron Beverly's 57-word-long title, read twice by the Chair (per Contest protocol) triggered wide audience laughter, helping him win second place honors.

Being Better

Craig Valentine[99] ended his speech with a pause —a huge pause—an unprecedented 12 seconds of silence.

Ed Tate[00] drew everyone's attention from the moment of his introduction: he stood center stage with a quiet warm smile engaging the audience with a much longer that normal 4-second pre-opening pause.

Morgan McArthur[93-2] uncovered a full-size horse replica (Title: The Difference is Horsepower) to conclude his speech.

Doing something better has great upside potential. Areas to consider include: smells, sounds and other senses used in speeches; silent words (where the word is mouthed (eg, the silence was —) or indicated by gesture (eg, point at heart for "inside me"); and IN Moments where you are IN the scene rather than just describing it.

Vulnerabilities

Isn't is strange that we always tend to hide our vulnerabilities—our failures, flaws, and frustrations? Yet, according to Craig Valentine, WCPS[99], it's when we share some of these aspects of our life we appear more human, more real, and more relatable—we are no longer that unapproachable, perfect, super-human speaker on the platform.

Another communicator[KP] even suggested if we don't have a limp, we should consider inventing one! She was serious. Mark Brown, WCPS[95], adds there should be a piece of you included in every speech. As much as your audience wants to hear you, they really want to *know* you.

Following are examples of how various speakers have allowed their audiences see behind their successful exterior. Consider how you, too, might gain by sharing some of your vulnerabilities.

According to my mother, I was too loud, I was too messy, and I was too clumsy to one day be a "lady." [16JL]

By the time I was in the 7th grade I was expelled twice. [RH]

Even though I wasn't where I wanted to be in life, I still had the time to make sure my life turned out okay. [14-2]

Every relationship started with great expectations—and ended in great depression. [15-3]

I achieved every single one of my goals. But I had no time. No time for my parents. No time for a vacation. No time for the present. And then it crashed—divorce. [10-3]

I became consumed by this dilemma and desperate for an answer. I turned to books, coaches, meditation—You name it I did it—I even searched in the bottom of a bottle of whiskey [09]

I came home running, crying from school because I had been teased and called names. [94-2]

I finally remembered that gift. I hate to admit it but it actually took me longer to untangle it from the grooves of my stapler than it did to get those pictures up on that computer screen. I immediately loved my computer gadget thingy and I regretted my reaction to my husband when I first received it. [16KH]

I know what it's like to not have enough money in your bank account. I know what it's like to worry when the bills start coming in … and I've been broken, lost and broke, many times in my life. [14]

I learned a very important lesson from Andy that day—that sometimes being right isn't always right. [14-2]

I took a $60,000 debt and in six short months—I doubled that debt—I turned my Subway sandwich shop into a non-profit organization. I financially fell on my face. [01]

I was 17 years old. I had already flunked high school and managed to get myself arrested. [14]

I was living in a small town in Indiana, I had a job I didn't like, I hadn't a date in three years and I had a couple of roommates named—Mom & Dad! … I moved to Los Angeles and started over! Six months later I had changed everything in my life but nothing had changed. [05]

I'm ashamed to say it now…[10]

My family was riddled with drugs and alcohol abuse. My nephew was murdered because he refused to join a gang. My best friend gave birth to a beautiful baby boy. I later discovered the father was my fiancé. My car was totaled and I had back injuries and was told I would never recover. Violated at the tender age of 16. Yet here I stand. [12-DP]

Now, how many of you are husbands in here? Raise your hands—Yeah!—I wasn't being unkind when I looked at my wife and said—*You know, those blue jeans look like they don't fit quite like they used to.*—Wow! Pain! Agony! Sleeping on the couch! [04RH]

Oh, there were precious moments where we actually looked into each other's eyes. I apologized for being mean on the trip.[14-3]

Raising my hand to shield my face from the scorching sun, or perhaps it was to wipe away the tears that were slowly rolling down my checks. [11AT]

She notices I'm starting to look a little goofy. Okay—goofier than usual. [01-LL]

The blame. The pain. The shame. I wanted to commit suicide… [15EB]

The previous day I was hopeless, I was defeated I was fired. I didn't want to spoil my family's fun …so I bore the weight of disappointment alone. Depressed, disgusted and downtrodden I contemplated my future. [04-3]

Then it struck me … I was chained by fears—waiting to die. No money, not really in love, no achievement to be proud of. I was wasting my life—and I knew it. [01-3]

Two years ago was the worst day of my life. I found myself standing at the edge of a pier looking out into the water, wondering if anyone would miss me if I jumped. [15-JJ]

What looked like a rosy future crumbled into a barren wasteland of shattered dreams, living feelings of despair, worry, and regret. [10-3]

When I quit my bartender's job, I went on tour with a stripper for the summer. I wrote home weekly to lessen parental concerns—it was a comic exposé of exposeurs. [93-RS]

When I was 22 an accident changed my view of the world completely. Before the accident I saw the world from an invincible 6 feet high. Now I see it from the height of the consummate navel gazer. In my new position—short and seated and recycled—I soon faced discrimination. [09]

Years ago I had many conversations with myself. Some contemplating my life, but unfortunately many of them were contemplating my death. … "I was sick and tired of being sick and tired." I had a dead-end job, a dead-end relationship, and a dead-end life … I needed help. [99]

You are 35, you are going nowhere, and you're broke. [Talking of himself] [10-2]

You say that I can't handle drugs
You know you may be right
I don't mean to upset you
I don't want to start a fight.
But once you start, it's hard to stop it
The truth is, I don't want to drop it.
I like to drink, I like to get high,
Don't worry about me—I'll get by
You say I won't, and if I don't
Just leave me—Let me die. [15-RD]
[Speaker sharing a dark poem written when a teenager]

Who Am I?

The best source of speech material is your own life. It is a composite of events, experiences, ideas and lessons with a unique viewpoint—yours. Your story is different from all others—and audiences are curious about the stories from your life's journey. Because it's different, no one else can talk with the same perspective as you. No one can contradict what you have experienced. Your life is a plethora of potential material awaiting transformation into speeches that others will enjoy hearing.

How do we remember all that's happened in our lives? We don't, but diverse memories from the past often run through the corridors of our minds. We should jot them down on anything handy and later include them in a personal *Who Am I* file. Over time, this becomes a growing collection of one or two sentence "remembrances of things past," of things that had some meaning to us—people, experiences, lessons, oddities, joys, regrets, warts and wonders—the framework of our existence. The entries are brief, but their few words recreate full meaningful images for us.

A selection of entries from my ever-growing *Who Am I* file is below. The file is one of the most valuable tools in my personal Speaker's Toolbox because its eclectic list of memories has triggered material for many speeches. In a sense, it's a highly abbreviated diary of your life that only you will fully understand.

As you read the following entries from my *Who Am I* file (from which many of my warts has been omitted for obvious reasons, but remain in my file), those entries that trigger the thought "I'd like to know more about that one" tells you how audiences will feel when you include in your speeches similar interesting pieces from your life.

Ancient Greece and Rome have become lifelong fascinations since visiting the Mediterranean in my 20s.

Antarctica—racing with whales

Antarctica—stillness—closest to God

As a kid, earned money (paper routes, lawns, garage, etc) for everything—no pocket money from parents

As kid played prisoner-of-war camps

Aunt Mary–when 13, gave me *Think & Grow Rich*—expanded my mind

Before graduating, discussed with Bishop about becoming a priest

Boxed (not well) in early teens

Cancer—Malignant—at 20

Cancer—my 5 wishes if I lived

Co-founded University Political Party Club

Coincidence: met a person at bullfight in Madrid and again two weeks later at top of St. Peter's.

Cyril Watson—""Don't need a suitcase to carry a good education with you"

Dan Bacon—"oldest teenager in town"—priceless advice giver

David Duggan—met in my 20's—wisest man I have ever known

Discovered when my High School friends changed so did my grades

El Greco—the day I discovered my favorite painter

Fiona—Disney every half birthday

Fiona—each birthday gave an influential book with an explanation

Fiona—felt I am but a link from Adam

First car—accident—speed—thought I was Sterling Moss

High School punishment—caning

High school—so scared of mandatory speech contests my mother would write each—I read it hurriedly and poorly

Ida D…taught me religious tolerance

Ina Smith—employee—lost her note of recognition—asked her manager to ask me for another—a big lesson for me.

Introduced to snowflakes and Outer Space about same time—new diverse directions for my mind to wander.

Joined Toastmasters at 22 when it began in New Zealand.

Looking across plane aisle and seeing a stranger reading book I had written!

Lost loveable Rosie, our Lhasa Apso

Mac, first year University roommate, taught me how to study effectively

Major mentors in business: THAC, BHP, DSR, NK; and then RWK & TES. Outstanding businessmen whose lessons will never end

Majored in accounting, economics and marketing, yet my economic history class taught me most about life and concern for the *common man*

Met Norman Rockwell; Peter Drucker

Missed Baker Scholar Award by one Excellent grade—real disappointment

My goal of arriving at meetings exactly on time was inspired by my favorite novel, *The Count of Monte Cristo*

Nearly drowned—saved by sharks

Nicolaes Maes—*Old Woman Praying* (before a simple meal)—Rijksmuseum

Ozymandias—read aloud this favorite High School sonnet 30 years later at the actual ruins site on the Nile

Paper route as kid—biggest lesson—when collecting the fortnightly dues, seeing the diversity in how people act, live, and maintain their homes

Played parceling as kids—tricked drivers

Played rugby, cricket, hockey, tennis while at High School

Postcards from diverse parts of world (when very young) from Aunt Gladys gave me a love of the world, travel, and stamps

Serendipitously came across Yeats' *Lake Isle of Innisfree* (a poem from High School) while in Ireland

Slept on kitchen floor in Greece (on my $5-a-day travels)

Squibby McG—mouth washed out with soap by nun for his swearing—taught me never to swear

Sunsets in Indonesia and Santorini

The loss of my older brother

Toastmaster in clubs in New Zealand, Ireland, IN, OH, NC, SC, and TN

Traveled around Ireland—my father-in-law and I judged each town by its Irish Coffee

Visited an Old Persons Home (age 8)—ever since it's been a very sad memory

Week long fast—nothing but water

You can't have should have … Dwyer

Zak Saba—superstitious—stayed in bed every Fri 13th—and died there on that day.

Xtra Tips

Over the years, I have enjoyed attending seminars by the WSC Champions and listening to their CDs and DVDs. I inhaled their snippets of wisdom—drawn from their "scar-tissue research" as they learned the craft of communicating on the way up to win their World Championship trophies.

The following are a few of them. Many reinforce ideas expressed elsewhere in the Toolbox, while the others complement them. As experience is the best teacher, be guided by what they have generously shared with others.

The Journey of a Speaker

Initially, most speakers are self-centered so that they are nervous about themselves—Will I remember the lines? Do I look good, sound good? How's my language? What techniques should I be thinking about? Do I have the right phrases? Are gestures right? Then, later, experience takes over and you move to a different level. It moves from "me" to "the audience." Your over-arching goal becomes: How can I serve the audience? What can I share from my experiences and insights to serve them? To help lift them? Speaking is a journey—you learn who you are; you become comfortable standing in front of audiences and share "stuff" (your stuff) to help them. MMc

You

Be different; be memorable MA^

Don't stand on the stage: own it. CV

Speak with conviction and sincerity, enthusiasm and vitality RF^

You & Your Audience

The audience wants to know you even more than they want to hear you. Let them learn something about you. MB

Show your ability by showing your vulnerability. Let people see you are human, that you are one of them—that you aren't up there on the platform above them all. MA^

Be conversational: re-live your speech moments, as in a conversation, shaking your head, gesticulating, etc. DL

Your Message

Have only one clear simple message, not two or three. RA

Like Clara in Wendy's ad "Where's the beef?" the audience rightly asks—"Where's the message?" RF^

What touches us in our lives is what touches the audience. Use it. MMc

Deliver the message, not the words. Avoid memorizing your speech word for word. Of course, write and practice your speech many times until it flows smoothly … but your priority is to connect with the audience by delivering the message rather than the words VJ

You can have a winning message; but does the winning message have you? OW

Burning Building Test: You have just discovered the building is on fire. Could you go out on stage and tell everyone the building was on fire? Of course! Why? Because you believe this is very important. And you can give a passionate clear message on other issues, too! Ask yourself: is your speech message as important or as compelling as "The room's on fire!!!" LM

Content and Stories

Say something the audience hasn't heard before. Get personal. Tell own life's stories and examples. These are yours and yours alone. No chance of any other speaker using same story. [DB]

A key advantage of telling your own stories is that you can re-live them rather than tell them. And the best stories are often the little ones. [RH]

The most important thing people want to hear about are your unique experiences—your business experiences [list them…]; your achievements [list them]; the adversities you have overcome [list them]; your serious hobbies [list them]…all relevant speech material. [DL]

Give your characters names; give them a little characteristic to picture them better, eg, his well-tailored blue suit. Remember we can't care about characters we can't see. [CV]

Create images to help audience see the scene, eg, My call wouldn't go through—nine digits separated me from sanity—I blacked out! [RH]

Write your speech; then examine every sentence. Ask: (1) So what? and (2) How can I make it clearer? [DL]

Speech Preparation & Practice

Prepare your speech not until you are sick of it but until you are in love with it and you want to share it. [DB]

The first 3-5 times, drill your speech out loud as though you are giving it on stage [ie, not in your head or as a whisper]. Do not stop for mistakes or corrections—you are practicing your idea flow, not seeking word perfection. The following time do it 6-10 times, etc. Later, speed-drill your speech—say it out loud as fast as you can to enhance memorization; then start it

at different points. This allows you, later, to focus on the audience and not on the speech. [LM]

Feedback (Two Different Approaches)

One WSC states before meeting he has put some brand-new material in his speech (without explaining what it is). Then explains that the feedback he seeks is answers to two questions regarding the whole speech: What do you like? What do you think should be improved? [LM]

Another prefers to ask specifics, eg, how did you feel at the end? Were there any parts where you mind wandered? This approach helps him understand why the audience may not be there with you: he may learn it was because of, say, comprehension or emotion. [VJ]

Try both. See what works for you.

Some Practical Points

Pause before starting speech. Scan the audience. Be there "in the moment." [DL]

Avoid introducing new material or stories towards the end of your speech; better to reinforce what you have already said. [JK]

Have a contingency plan in case the red light comes on sooner than expected. [JK]

Mark * for an audience chuckle and * * for a laugh in your speech draft (to help estimate your speech length). [JK]

Speech health: suck lemons a lot; drink tons of water; rest voice; speak from diaphragm. [OW]

Darren LaCroix's essentials:

1. The Pause. Use it to make your audience think, to touch their heart, and to make sure the audience is with you. Pause until they're uncomfortable; get comfortable with the silence during a pause.
2. Understand that you don't have to be perfect.
3. Connect with the audience. Remember the Jerry McGuire concept: Have them at "hello."

Speeches to Learn From

You have reviewed many of the basic tools that help build better speeches. Now it's time to move from pieces of speeches to total speeches to understand how speakers have thoughtfully and carefully fitted them together in a beautiful audible jigsaw puzzle.

Rather than offer an array of speeches of past champions, I have chosen to show the different speeches required of just three speakers on their journey to become Toastmasters International World Champion of Public Speaking®. Reading their speeches will show you that great speakers are not "one-trick ponies" but craft and deliver excellent speeches on diverse topics.

Each Toastmasters Contest speech has to be excellent because today about 30,000 Toastmasters from over 140 countries enter the annual knockout series leading to the world title. The odds of winning are astronomical: each person emerging from 30,000 entrants has about a 0.003% chance!

Prior to 2010, three completely different speeches were required in this journey: one at District (about 150 Clubs), one at Regional (or Semifinals), and another on the "Big Stage" (the final 10 speakers). In 2010, the requirement was changed to two completely different speeches, one at the Semifinals, and another on the "Big Stage" two days later, both held at the annual convention of Toastmasters International®.

The selection includes the speeches of three champions:

2010	David Henderson
2007	Vikas Jhingran
2004	Randy Harvey

You will quickly see the clarity of their messages and the many tools with which they used to deliver them, including Alliteration, Connecting, Contrast, Details, Emotion, Exaggeration, Humor, Metaphors, Senses, Similes, Triples, Twists, and Visual Words.

Following the champions' speeches are three other favorites of mine. On the lighter side, they will not only create chuckles but are worthy of study, for humorous speeches, too, can be examples of excellence. The speakers are:

Jay Nodine

George Vest

Noah Sweat

The Best Medicine
~ David Henderson ~
2010 Semifinal Winner
Toastmasters World Championship of Public Speaking®

(Enters wearing doctor's coat with child's stethoscope, pager, etc., attached)

The best doctor in the whole wide world
Does more than stitch up cuts, push pills, or take out tonsils.
He gives people hope.

Madame Contest Chair, fellow Toastmasters,
Hope is the best medicine—
Because you can't always cure people.
But you can give them strength to push on—
And that's what hope does.
It gives you strength even when you're dying.

Miss Mamo was obviously dying.
She had lots of tubes
Tubes to her wrist
Tubes to her nose—
Tubes to this big machine
That went beep, beep.
She had thick, beautiful hair once
But it was all gone
And so were all the relationships she took for granted.
Now she accepted dying from cancer
Because she had to
But no one can accept dying alone
Without hope
And they don't have to.
They just need help from the best doctor in the whole wide world.

Now this doctor became a doctor in 1981
At the age of 6
When he got a Fisher Price medical kit for his birthday
And his mom told him—

"Since you want to be a doctor so bad
You can bring your little butt to work with me
And take care of a real patient."
Now—yes—the doctor had had a few mishaps
So this time mama picked the patient—Miss Mamo.
You see the boy's mother was a nurse in the ICU
Which—by the way—never made much sense to him.
Every time somebody asked about it—he said—
"I see you too."
But, I'm digressing—

What the boy remembered most
About his first visit to the ICU—
Was the smell.
It smelled like somebody threw up
Or somebody's puppy had an accident
And whoever cleaned it
Used buckets and buckets of Pine Sol
To try to hide the smell.

But, fellow Toastmasters,
No matter how hard grown-ups try
They can't hide the stench of despair—
Or suffering—or hopelessness—from children.
By the time that boy got to Miss Mamo's room,
He didn't want to be a doctor any more
Especially not when his mom told him to go inside all by himself.
"I don't want to," he told her.
"Why not?"
"Because she's scary looking. She's bald-headed."
"Boy—you'd better hold your voice down."
"I'm serious, Mom. I'm just a kid. You're a nurse—you go."
"I tried to, but I can't."
And she cried until the little boy said—
"I'm sorry, Mommy. I'll go."
And Miss Mamo must have known that boy was coming
Because as soon as she saw him
Her eyes got really big like it was Christmas
And she said
"Oooh, sweet Baby Jesus."
But I said,

"No, I'm your doctor."
"Well, of course, you are, Baby.
What kind of medicine did you practice?"
"My mom says I'm a good doctor
So I don't think I have to practice.
Let's have a look—shall we?
Can you take a deep breath
And blow out all the candles
Just like this [breathes in and out].
Again [breathes in and out].
Good.
Now open really wide and go Aaah.
Again.
Aaah.
Excellent—Your heart is beating 55 miles per hour—
That's normal.
Your breath is a little stinky,
But it's nothing to worry about.
May I see your arm please?
[Pretends to give an injection]
If those wear off
I want you to take two Hershey's kisses
And call me in the morning.
[Toy pager buzzes.]
They're paging me. I have to go."

And, fellow Toastmasters, he did go—
Every day that entire summer.
The boy went inside.
His mom stayed outside.
And for the first time in a long time Miss Mamo was hopeful.
She went from waiting to die to dying to live—
Each day—
For one more visit from the best doctor in the whole wide world.
Until one day during a routine visit Miss Mamo went "ugh"
[Put his hand to his chest]
And that machine that goes beep, beep
Starts going beep, beep, beep, beep, beep, beep, beep, beep
And a nurse rushed in … beep, beep, beep
And a doctor rushed in
And when it seemed like that machine couldn't beep any faster

Or Miss Mamo's face couldn't get any tighter
Something happened that our young doctor simply wasn't prepared for.
His mom walked in the room.
She knelt down by Miss Mamo,
And she took her hand.
Miss Mamo tried to talk
But the boy's mother just said
"Sshhh. I know you love me"—
"And I love you too."

Fellow Toastmasters,
Sometimes a single act of forgiveness changes everything.
Miss Mamo relaxed.
She looked peaceful.
And that machine went *beeeeeeeeeeeeeep*
[Draws a straight line with his hand].
Confused, sad, and scared,
Our young doctor melted into a corner.
A nurse took him [help hand] and said
"She left something for you—a letter."

And, fellow Toastmasters,
Would you believe—almost thirty years later—
I still have it [takes a letter out of his pocket].
It reads—

Dear Doctor David,
I never properly introduced myself.
My name is Joyce Janik Cunio
And I'm your grandmother.
As you get older
Keep in mind there's only one thing you cannot find again
Once you have lost it—
Lost time.
I lost six years of your life
Because I abandoned your mother—
A mistake I thought was as incurable as cancer
Until a young doctor taught me I didn't need a cure—
I needed hope.
I was able to endure my suffering because my grandson—
The best doctor in the whole wide world—

Brought me kisses every day.
I love you, David.
Always,
Miss Mamo.

I don't know if I could do what my mom did—
But I sure am glad she did it.
Fellow Toastmasters,
Hope is the best medicine
So if you have lost touch with someone who needs it
Then write them a prescription before it is too late.

Madame Contest Chair.

The Aviators

~ David Henderson ~

2010 Winner
Toastmasters World Championship of Public Speaking®

(Enters wearing aviator costume—cap, goggles, bomber jacket, etc.)

In 1983—the two best pilots in Texas teamed up to fight the Red Baron.
We called ourselves the Aviators.
[Sound of plane flying.]
"Snoopy one to Snoopy two—I see him.
Break hard right.
Tighten your britches.
I'm coming in hot.
[Sound of plane's gun.]
Woo-hoo!"

Mr. Contest Chair, fellow Toastmasters, it was official.
We flew a bazillion combat missions with zero causalities.
We were invincible.
So we thought.
Truth is we were too young to know
That sooner or later
We all fall down.
That's the bad news.
The good news is no matter how badly you fall
Love can lift you back up.

I met my first love in kindergarten.
Every kid had a job during recess.
We were cops and robbers,
Cowboys and Indians,
Barbies and Kens.
No two kids had the same job
Which was most apparent the one day each year
We wore our professional attire to school—
Halloween.
I had the costume contest in the bag
Until Jackie Parker walked in—
In a Snoopy aviation costume

Just like mine—
Except she had moves like a runway model.
I thought I heard music,
But it was just the rhythm of my heart.
I looked at her and my eyes pooped out of my head.
She looked at me the way my mom looked at my dad
After he forgot their anniversary.
Fellow Toastmasters,
Not only was I dressed like Snoopy
I was in the doghouse.
Jackie walked up to me and said
"Oh no, you didn't!"
"Are you mad we have on the same outfit?"
"No...yes...maybe."
I learned something that day.
Girls don't mind when you show up wearing the same outfit.
They mind when you show up looking better in the same outfit.
You see in addition to my helmet, goggles and bomber jacket,
I had a real silk scarf and Jackie didn't.
For some reason I didn't know then
And I don't know now
I gave my scarf to Jackie.
She won the contest—
But I won her over.

After that we were the Aviators,
And we were invincible.
But sooner or later,
We all fall down.
When Jackie fell and hurt her elbow,
It seemed like no big deal at first.
She took too long getting back up.
No big deal.
Her arm took too long to heal.
No big deal.
Until the doctor said she had a bone infection.
That was a big deal.
The reason why was even bigger.
Jackie had sickle-cell anemia,
Which meant our flying days were over.

Many of you are wondering the same thing I was.
What's sickle cell?
It's a genetic blood disorder.
People think of it as an African American disease,
But it affects people all over the world
From the Middle East to Asia to South America.
People with sickle cell have deformed red blood cells
Which carry oxygen through your blood vessels.
Normal cells look like disks
And pass freely through your blood cells.
Sickle cells look like sickles.
They clump together causing traffic jams
Which in turn cause episodes.
First you're fine, and then you're in pain,
And then you're fine, and then you die.
There is no known cure.

I'm ashamed to say it now,
But when my mom told me that,
I questioned what's the point in loving somebody,
I mean truly loving somebody
When you know they're going to die?
And fellow Toastmasters
I will never forget my mom putting her hands on my shoulders
Looking me in the eyes and saying
"Baby, losing people is part of loving people.
When it happens it isn't up to you.
All you get to choose is what you do with the time you have.
Now that little girl needs you by her side
And hard as it is going to be
You need to be there
Or you will regret it for the rest of your life;
And trust me
Regretting is a lot harder than loving.
So you be strong and you make me proud."

They diagnosed Jackie when she was 7
And she died when she was 14 years old.
And through those years

I found the strength to follow my mom's advice.
Through every episode I stuck by Jackie's side.
And in the end
I decided to say good-bye the same way we said hello.
I dusted off my helmet and wore it to the hospital.
You should have seen the look on Jackie's face when I asked her
"Do you remember how we first met?"
And she said
"No, yes, maybe."

And what she did next
Made me regret ever wondering
Whether it's worth it loving somebody
When you know they're going to die.
She reached in her nightstand,
As she pulled out that scarf.
And I said—"You kept that thing?"
She said,
"Not the thing, David, the memory.
When my pain got to where I couldn't bear it,
I went back to the moment you gave this to me
And it got me through.
Your love, it got me through.
I hope giving it back does the same thing for you."

Sooner or later, we all fall down.
I've fallen down many times since then
But remembering Jackie always lifts me back up.
Fellow Toastmasters
Losing people is part of loving people
But if you do it right
They'll never leave your side even after they're gone.

Mr. Contest Chair.

Perfect

~ Vikas Jhingran ~

**2007 District Winner
Toastmasters World Championship of Public Speaking®**

Let me ask you a question that may seem a little strange—
"How many of you chose your parents?
How about your kids?
(Some of you wish you had!)
Or your health problems?
No—they just happened.
My point is
That whether we like it or not
"Everything in life is arranged".

Mr Contest Master, fellow toastmasters,
Today I'm going to tell you about a time
When something in my life was arranged
How that changed my life
And how the lesson that I learnt will change your life too.

It was 2001
Houston Texas
And I
Having noticed the number of girls showing interest in me—
Had bowed to tradition.
Yes, friends,
I was going to have an arranged marriage.

I immediately discovered an unexpected benefit—
It's a fantastic conversation starter.
Just walk into a party and casually mention
That you are going to have an arranged marriage
And see how the room is transformed.

For the next 30 minutes,
You will become the center of all attention
People will be fighting to get a glimpse of you—
To make sure you actually exist.

108

In spite of all the attention,
I was very scared.
Was this the right thing to do?
Should I wait till I find the "right girl"?
Or should I let my parents in India find one for me?

One day, with these thoughts swirling in my mind,
I decided to give my mother a call.
"Hey mom, how are you going about looking for a girl for me?"
"Don't worry Vikas.
This is my job.
I look at many things—
Like the photograph."
"Yeah,
And you consider only the most beautiful ones—right"
"No, no, Vikas—
A boy and a girl should look good together."
(Terror in my eyes as I look at my face in a mirror)
"You've got to change this rule mom"—
"Vikas, this is my job.
You just relax."

After several such 'confidence boosting' conversations
Mom and dad found a girl and surprisingly—
I liked her.
Mom did break her rule though—
Anjali was charming and beautiful—
In fact so beautiful
That for once I was sure that arranged marriage was the way to go.

Finally the day of the wedding arrived.
Three days of dancing and singing.
With hundreds of people—
Most of whom I did not know and will never see again.
Countless ceremonies.
It was quite an event
And by the time it was over
I had just one thought in mind
"I am never going to do this again."
No wonder the divorce rate in India is so low—
People will put up with anything
To avoid going through the wedding again.

After the wedding
Anjali and I flew back to Texas—
But I was still confused.
Anjali was beautiful, educated, and cultured.
She was perfect for me—
Or was she?
What if she was not the right one?
What if I would have found the "Perfect girl" if had I just waited?
What if?

Friends, a few weeks into my marriage
I had been poisoned …
Poisoned by the "what if" question.
And this doubt and regret
Started to choke the very meaning out of my life—
Because—you see
Instead of strengthening my new marriage
I was already regretting it …
Until one day I was watching TV
And some crazy guy came on and said
"Everything in life is arranged … "
And I jumped up and said
"You better believe it!"

Now, wait a minute, Ladies and gentlemen,
Don't tell me you don't argue with your TV—
You, know what the best part about it is—
You always win
Because if you are losing
You can shut if off and walk away.
Then this crazy man carried on
"Everything in life is arranged—
Until you make it perfect."
"What do you mean?" I shouted.
The man continued
"You don't choose the country you were born in
Or the color your skin
Or the relatives you have to deal with everyday
But you have the choice to make things perfect."
That day—

For the first time—
I lost an argument with my TV.
But I realized
That if I wanted to have a perfect life
I won't get it by asking "what if"—
I had to take whatever I had—
And make it right.

Today, five years later,
My wife and I have a beautiful marriage—
Today our arranged marriage is—
Perfect.

Friends, I don't know what life has to offer next—
And it may be way out of line
But there is no reason to fret and whine
For though you didn't cause your sorry plight
You do have the power to make it right

After all
Everything in life is arranged—
Until you make it perfect.

Postcard

~ Vikas Jhingran ~

2007 Semifinal Winner
Toastmasters World Championship of Public Speaking®

"Have you seen the Taj Mahal?" Jamie asked.
I was used to this question.
As soon as someone found out I was from India
This was the second question they asked me—
The first one always being
"Did you have an arranged-marriage?"
And so I had a prepared answer.
"Isn't it beautiful?" I replied.
The truth was that I had not seen the Taj Mahal
But I was too embarrassed to admit it—
So I learnt to describe it from a postcard.

Mr. Contest Master, fellow Toastmasters,
And anyone who claims to have seen a monument based on a postcard—
It works!
I had a great discussion with Jamie about the Taj Mahal
But this was the straw that broke the camel's back.
Two years ago when my wife and I visited India
We planned a trip to the Taj Mahal.

Both of us were so excited.
We told everyone about it—
All our relatives and friends knew we were going to the Taj Mahal.
When my favorite Uncle Jay found out we were going to the Taj Mahal
He had just one piece of advice—
"Be careful of pickpockets.
They are like magicians.
They could get your wallet out even when you had your hand on it."
And not just him—
All my aunts and cousins said the same thing—
So when I was at the Taj Mahal
That's all I could think about.
In fact, every thirty seconds
My hand would automatically drift to my back pocket

Just to make sure that my wallet was there.
That afternoon, while standing in line to buy a drink
I got engrossed in a discussion with my wife and our guide
And just for a few minutes my mind was wandered—
And when my hand went back—
My wallet was gone.

How could this be?
I had been so careful.
I turned around and shouted
"Someone stole my wallet!"
In just an instant the hundred or so people around us were galvanized—
Their eyes darting from one corner to another for anything suspicious—
The thief could not be far.
As I was desperately looking around
I heard the voice of my driver "Sirji, Sirji"
"What?" I shouted.
"It's in your hand!"
And sure enough it was in my hand.
I immediately realized what had happened.
I had taken it out to buy the drink
And when my other hand touched my pocket
I immediately assumed that someone stole it—
Because that's what I had been thinking about the whole time.

I can never forget this incident because of two reasons—
One—my wife won't let me forget it—
It has too much entertainment value for her
And second because of how I felt that evening.
I had just spent the day
In front of one of the most beautiful structures built by man—
But I couldn't recall the touch of the radiant, white marble
Or the elaborate carvings on the pillars.
I didn't remember
The smell of the flowers that surrounded the structure
Or the details of the spectacular dome.
It was almost like I had just seen a—postcard.

My day felt incomplete—
Like I had missed something
But it took a phone call to make me realize what.
It was the 15th of March last year.
It was early in the morning and the phone rang—

My mother was on the line.
"I have bad news Vikas.
Uncle Jay passed away".
I was shocked—
My favorite uncle—
Gone.
"But mom the doctor gave him six months
How could he be gone—"
"Well doctors can be wrong you know—"
"He can't be gone, mom."
"He's dead Vikas—
"But mom—I was almost done with my project;
I finally had some time to call him."
Tears rolled clown my cheeks
As I remembered the wonderful years
I had spent with him when I was a kid.
I saw myself playing in his small house in Calcutta,
Those hot summer days I spent playing in his backyard.
His caring hug—his gentle smile.
As these images raced across my mind
I realized for the first time
That I had lived my whole life like a—postcard.
Flat and incomplete.
I had always been so busy building the future
That I had never lived in the moment—
The moment that had the smell, the touch,
The sound and the emotion—
The moment that is gone in a snap—
Forever—just like uncle Jay was gone—
Forever.

Friends, there are too many of us
Who live our lives worrying about our wallet
And forget to enjoy the magnificence of the Taj Mahal in front of us—
Not realizing that if we fail to capture the moment—
The sound, the smell, the touch, and the feeling—
What remains is a picture without a soul
A memory without emotion
Just a postcard—
Your life is much more than a simple…postcard.

The Swami's Question

~ Vikas Jhingran ~

2007 Winner
Toastmasters World Championship of Public Speaking®

(Walks on stage with envelope in hand)

My hands were shaking
My throat was dry ...
In my hands was a letter [holding up envelope]
That was going to change my life ...
Would it be for better ...
Or worse? ...
The answer was inside.

I stared at the return address
Massachusetts Institute of Technology ...
The Graduate School of my dreams.
Would it begin with "Congratulations" ......
Or "You've got to be kidding!!!" ...
The answer was inside.

[Puts envelope in inside jacket pocket]
My mind drifted back to when it all began ...
Fourteen years ago.

Mr. Contest Master, fellow Toastmasters,
And anyone here who remembers being a teenager.
The year was 1989
I was a teenager and my parents were desperate...
Sounds familiar, doesn't it!!!
College was just a few years away and my grades ...
Not there.
My parents had been brilliant students ...
And clearly very trusting of each other
Because they ruled out any problems with my genes.
But having tried everything ...
From tutoring to mentoring
Pleading to threatening
They turned to the supernatural ...
The Swami.

One afternoon
Mom and I traveled to the old part of the city of Calcutta, India.
Here the houses were so close that sunlight was a myth …
The aroma of spices
Drifted in the hot, humid air
And here in a small hut
Sat the holy man everyone called the Swami.
His saffron robe drenched in sweat.
He tried to solve the problems people put before him.
"Swami, Vikas has lot of potential …
But the grades are not good" my mother pleaded …
To which the Swami replied
"Meditation—try meditation."
And in a flash
His attention was on the next person.

I really did not believe in this meditation stuff
But one look at my mom …
(Look at her and show a frightened look)
And I knew I would have to give it a try …
But then I got hooked.
Did you know that meditation is cool?"
Yeah … when my friends found out that I was into meditation
My popularity shot up like Apple's stock.
I was really enjoying all the attention …
But behind closed doors
My meditation practice was in trouble …
Sitting in a quiet room with my eyes closed should be easy …
Except I could not stay awake.
Within a few moments of closing my eyes
I was sleeping like a baby …
But meditation had made me so popular
That I had to find a way around it.

So mom and I went back to the Swami …
"Ask yourself question—who are you?"
Have you ever looked at modern art and wondered …
So which side is up?
My visit to the Swami was equally confusing.
Over the next few months
I tried to answer the Swami's question …
And miraculously my grades improved so much

That I was accepted into a good undergraduate program in India.
Freshman year of college—
What's not to love about it?
Meditation was out and in came ... girls!!!
Then came my first semester grades ...
It felt like life had kicked me in the stomach so hard
That I was left gasping for air
And begging for answers.
And in the months that followed
My desperate attempts to bounce back
Only made me question my own abilities.

Until one day, tired, frustrated,
I closed my eyes and returned to the Swami's question ...
"Who are you?"
And in that deep silence
I heard the music of my dreams
The song of my talents
The symphony of my spirit ...
And I finally understood what the Swami had done ...
Meditation was just a tool
To make me stop and listen
Because the answer was not out there ...
The answer was inside.

Fourteen years later
Once again the answer had been inside.
[Takes envelope from pocket]
It did begin with congratulations! ...
I had fulfilled my dream ...
All because the Swami showed me that the answer
Is not in that magic pill—or with Dr. Phil
The answer is always—inside.

Friends, have you ever looked inside? ......
What if the answer to your problems is not outside?
What if your answer [silent—just hands on chest indicating "is inside"]?

What the Swami asked me then
I ask you now—
"Who are you?"

Sticks and Stones Will Break Your Bones But Words Will Never Hurt You—It's A Lie!

~ Randy Harvey ~

2004 District Winner
Toastmasters World Championship of Public Speaking®

Sticks and stones will break your bones
But words will never hurt you.
It's a lie!!!!
Fellow Toastmasters and guests,
Nothing—could be further from the truth.
Can you think of anything
That wounds so deeply and lasts so long
As hurtful words?

I experienced it in my life.
As a kindergartener
I remember moving from school to school
Because my father
Had just gotten out of prison for armed robbery.
And with each new school came new words—
Loser, convict's kid, half-breed.
Hurtful words.
And what is it about humankind
That takes the hurt that people inflict on us
And inflicts it on other people?

I remember in 6th grade
Standing in the 8th grade hallway
And looking down the hallway.
And there was Gina Greenstein.
My friend poked me in the ribs and says
"Gina Greenstein."
Now Gina, she was a big girl—a really big girl.
Being a 6th grade boy I said
"Gina, you fat cow."
My friends immediately started laughing
But what I saw were those brown, wounded eyes welling with tears.
And my heart was struck like an anvil.
My conscience cried out, "Foolishness."
The next thing I heard was Shana yelling—
"Watch out, Gina's coming."

I looked up and there were red, raging eyes with fists clinched
And she was bearing down on me.
I woke up.
I spun around and wham, wham—
Hit Sam Wilson's belt buckle right in the forehead—
Now, he was the assistant principal.
As I lay on the floor looking up at Sam
Who was as tall as a house
He leaned over and helped me up—
By my right ear.
As I stood at that chalkboard
With my nose in the circle and my arms outstretched
Breathing chalk dust
My calves were on fire and I was in agony.
But it was those brown eyes that were haunting me most.
That—
And the fact that I had to run from Gina for the next eight months.
Hurtful words.
Now how many of you are husbands in here?
Raise your hands. Yeah.
I wasn't being unkind when I looked at my wife and said
You know, those blue jeans look like they don't fit quite like they used to.
Wow!—Pain—Agony—Sleeping on the couch!

As a School Administrator when I entered my career
I was called to a Middle School in Springfield, Oregon.
And I sat across from the table from a rather chunky, troubled youth
And I looked into his eyes—dark eyes, empty eyes—
And he spoke venomous, cruel words at me
And I was afraid—afraid for two reasons.
First, it was like looking into a mirror as if I was 14 years old again
And second, I was fearful.

Two years later as the Director of Human Resources,
I was called to Thurston High School
And there across on the cafeteria floor was Kip Kinkel.
He had just killed 2 students and wounded 20 others.
It was my responsibility, along with another gentleman
To go around and take the names of the wounded and the dead
To give words of life and words of death
To parents across the street, at the church.
He was speaking words and no one was listening.
Solomon is thought by many to be the wisest man ever in our history.

He said:
"Death and life are in the power of the tongue."
"Death and life are in the power of the tongue."

Every day as I drive to work
There is a homeless person who stands by the stop sign
With a sign that says
Hungry—Feed Me.
Yet every day we go through our lives looking at people
And their faces cry out *Hungry—Feed me—Nourish my soul—*
And we pass on by.
The last I checked
Our tongue was attached to the back of our throat.
We have the ability to control it.
We have the ability to speak words of life into people
To encourage, to strengthen, to build up
Rather than tear down.
Do the people in your life
When they listen to you speak
Do they think mortician or physician?
Do they see you as a bleeder or a feeder?
Are you an investor or a divestor?
Are you venial or congenial?
It's all in your control.
You are the one
Who can make the difference in the lives of other people.
No one else.
John Holmes said—
"With one trifling exception, the entire universe is composed of others."
That's who our speech is directed toward.

Toastmasters, let me challenge you to take control
And give out words of life
To encourage those that you touch every day.
It's an investment you can make—
Without spending a dime.
It's interest you can draw—
Freely given.
You have the power—
Go forward! Give life!

Don't Settle for Greatness—
When You Can Be Immortal

~ Randy Harvey ~

2004 Semifinal Winner
Toastmasters World Championship of Public Speaking®

Begins singing

Hello, Mary Lou,
Goodbye heart.
Sweet Mary Lou,
I'm so in love with you.
I knew Mary Lou we'd never part.
So hello, Mary Lou, goodbye heart.

Mary Lou was my momma.
And up until the age of nine
I thought my daddy wrote that song.
When I came to breakfast singing that song
My momma would light up like fireworks on the 4th of July.

Mr. Contest Chair, fellow Toastmasters and guests,
It's important that you know my momma was an Immortal.
There are many good people in this world
And there are a few great people—
But there are very few Immortals.
Now you may not be able to tell by looking at me
But I was a naughty child.
By the time I was in the 7th grade
I was expelled twice.
The second time
Because of seven thumbtacks strategically placed
To get a rise out of my science teacher.
It was hilariously successful.
I laughed so hard it was difficult to deny my culpability.
My momma wasn't laughing though.
When I got home that night
I wasn't laughing either.
She treated me to a hickory stick waltz.

You know what I mean—
A piece of kindling taken from the wood box
Applied to the backside in steady rhythms.
You sing along in keys, chords, and crescendos.
True to form though,
Afterward, my momma wrapped her arms around me
And cradled my head in the crook of her neck
And held me until my tears subsided—
And the neighbor's dog stopped howling.

At dinnertime
As we sat there on those ugly orange Naugahyde chairs
I looked at her through the mystic steam
Rising off the roast beef, carrots, and potatoes.
I asked her–
"Momma, will I be a great man someday?"
At first I thought she didn't hear me.
And then she looked up with those watery brown eyes
That pierced my soul.
"Son, don't settle for greatness. Be immortal.
Great men seek their own interests
And the accolades of others like you did today."

 After my two-week thumbtack hiatus
I returned to school and there she was—
A true Immortal—
Mrs. Childers, my English teacher.
She took one look at me and said
"You are a rogue! And I like you already."
She collected every misfit, malcontent and miscreant
In the 7th grade
And for an entire year
Not a single one us got into trouble.
Not one, not once.
She loved us.
She cared for us.
She was so sly and cunning
That she got all of her 7th grade boys
To dress up in pink and purple leotards
Don tutus
And regale audiences with Shakespeare.
She was an Immortal.

I remembered going home at the end of my 7th grade year
Saying to my momma,
"Momma, Mrs. Childers is an Immortal.
I'm going to be a teacher."
She looked at me—
"Time will tell."

I remember the last conversation I had with my momma.
I had just finished college.
I was a new 5th grade teacher.
I had finished teaching a year.
I had kids that I loved.
I walked into my momma's hospital room and I said
"Hello, Mary Lou."
She said
"Are you great or immortal today?"
"Merely great, Mama."
We talked well into the evening—about life.
And she had to admit that Mrs. Childers was truly an Immortal
Because she had inspired in me
A passion for learning and literature and life.

Fifteen years later
I was standing in a gas station pumping gas
And this beat-up old Datsun pick-up
Screeched to a halt behind me.
Out jumped this lanky young man
And walked straight toward me.
I looked him in the eye—
I knew I didn't owe him any money.
He walked right up to me.
With my quizzical look
He knew I didn't know who he was.
Raising his voice, he said
"Do you remember grabbing me
Standing me on a desk
And auctioning me off as a slave?"
He smiled.
"Brent Larson! You were in my very first 5th grade class."
"I certainly was and I've been looking for you.
I want you to know I'm a teacher today
At this high school right over here because of you.

You made a difference in my life."
Well, there we were—
Two grown men
Crying and hugging each other in a gas station
As the local "lookie-loos" drove by and stared.

As I drove the 70 miles to my conference
I wept.
I wanted so much to go back to that hospital room
And have that conversation again with my mama.
You see, I became an Immortal that day.
In the embrace of Brent Larsen
I realized I had made a difference in a child
Now making differences in the lives of other children.

It all began
With the Immortal teacher, Mrs Childers
Who put the fire in my soul to touch the lives of kids.
And the words of my Mama—
"Don't Settle for Greatness—
When You Can Be Immortal."

Lessons from Fat Dad
~ Randy Harvey ~
2004 Winner
Toastmasters World Championship of Public Speaking®

[These are the speaker's actual formatted speech practice notes. Omitted are the choreography side notes and the three different colors of print.]

When I was seven,

we drove to my cousin's for dinner

—and, to show off my Fat Dad's new car—

a 1960 Ford Fairlane.

I fell asleep on the backseat.

My folks went to the house and left me sleeping.

When I woke up,

I stumbled out of the car and headed for the porch.

Woof.

OWWWOOO.

I WAS surrounded by a pack of black and tan hunting hounds.

OWWWOOO!!

My heart jumped.

Then so did I:

To the trunk and then the roof

of that new car.

Mr. Contest Chair, fellow toastmasters.

Frozen like a treed raccoon, I was screaming and bawling <PAUSE> the hounds was howling and circling.

AN UGLY ONE-EYED DOG CLAWED AND SCRATCHED HIS WAY ONTO THE TRUNK, HIS YELLOW TEETH SNAPPING AND FOAMING. <PAUSE>

I WAS STANDING IN WATER—IT WAS MINE!

HIS CLAWS SCREECHED AND SLIPPED ON THE GLASS WHEN I
HEARD-- "SON!!"
I DOVE AT THE VOICE!

And was caught in Fat Dad's arms.

Safety was a flannel shirt that smelled of CHERRY tobacco and
a BELLOW, SCATTERING hounds like cottonseed ON the wind.

The next morning as Fat Dad tried to buff the scratches from his new car . . .
I said -- I'M SORRY FAT DADY YOU HAD TO RESCUE ME
He scooped me up in his big arms.
In life, sometimes you're the catcher,
Sometimes you're the caught.
When you love somebody, their trouble is your trouble--
The lesson--was love.

•

Fat Dad was my DADDY—AND THAT loving nickname, Fat Dad, HAS
BEEN handed down THROUGH FOUR GENERATIONS of men IN MY
FAMILY.

•

When I was sixteen Fat Dad bought me a 63 Volkswagen beetle: gray, wide
tires, chrome wheels, and bucket seats.
I was driving one sunny afternoon,
 singing to Simon and Garfunkel on my eight track—
"Cecelia you're breaking my heart",
A HUMUNGOUS HORSEFLY SHOT THROUGH THE WINDOW, IN MY MOUTH, AND DOWN
MY THROAT.
IT CAME BACK UP—LODGED IN MY RIGHT NOSTRIL.
WHAT WOULD YOU DO WITH A HORSEFLY BUZZING IN YOUR NOSE--TAKING BITES THE
SIZE OF TEXAS?
I STEERED WITH MY KNEES AND TRIED TO FIRE THAT BUG OUT MY NOSE.
THE CAR SWERVED TO THE LEFT,

THEN CATAPULTED RIGHT,

CUT DOWN THE MORISON'S FENCE—SAILING THROUGH THEIR YARD--AIMED STRAIGHT

AT MOSSBURGER'S FOUNTAIN,

WHERE MARY POPPINS STOOD—HOLDING HER UMBRELLA—

POURING WATER FROM A CAN.

I HIT THAT FOUNTAIN SO HARD I LAUNCHED HER LIKE SPUTNIK-- MARY POPPINS HOV-

ERED BRIEFLY OVER THE RIVER, <PAUSE>

THEN WENT DOWN FASTER THAN A SPOONFUL OF SUGAR! <pause>

The Morison's and the Mossburgers were a bit excited.

Not Fat Dad.

He rode in like the cavalry and made peace with the Neighbors.

I was sitting on a rock in shock—as Fat Dad put his arm around me I burst in to tears.

 "Shssssh--We'll fix the fence,<pause> I'll buy another fountain, <pause> we'll even replace the Ol' car--those are just things."   "But, I can't replace you." <pause>

"Besides, the town will talk about this for weeks."   -----The lesson was love.

•

Teenage boys don't always think about cars—Sometimes they think about— GIRLS!

Fat Dad overheard me and my BUDDIES BRAGGING about our adventures with WOMEN!

Not being the shy type, he joined right in--listened for a while,

then like a bucket of cold water in a hot shower said:

"Boys—real men love for a lifetime, not for a moment." <PAUSE>

 Ruined the whole conversation!

FAT DAD LOVED MY MAMA. When they walked in the garden or sat on the sofa their hands seemed to find each other.

When Mama watched TV, Fat Dad would wrap his arms around her and rest his chin on her shoulder KISS HER ON THE CHEEK.

OOH, I COULDN'T BELIEVE OLD PEOPLE CARRIED ON LIKE THAT.

Fat Dad's love for my Mama was more than romance. WHEN MAMA battled A CANCER THAT EVENTUALLY TOOK HER LIFE, FAT Dad LIKE A good shepherd nursing a wounded lamb: bathed <PAUSE>, fed <PAUSE> read—and sang to her. <PAUSE>

When MY MAMA'S SUNSET came, and TURNED TO STARLIGHT, Fat Dad held her close—Whispered words of LOVE <PAUSE> WORDS OF FAITH <PAUSE>—to calm her fear.

Fat Dad's love for MY Mama was a gift to my wife and children. WATCHING HIM I LEARNED HOW TO LOVE THEM FOR A LIFETIME. The lesson? LOVE.

THIS YEAR I HAD MY first Father's day without Fat Dad. I MISS HIM. But his lessons have prepared me for a lifetime of love: < PAUSE>
1.	When you love, <PAUSE>sometimes you're the catcher and sometimes you're the caught <PAUSE>
2.	When there's trouble, Love rushes in, wraps its strong arms around you<pause>
3.	REAL MEN—WELL<PAUSE> THEY LOVE FOR A LIFETIME <PAUSE> NOT FOR A MOMENT.

FELLOW TOASTMASTERS—THE LESSON IS LOVE—AND **TODAY MY HEART OVERFLOWS–WHEN MY CHILDREN CALL ME "FAT DAD."**

The Golden Years—Yeah! Right!

~ Jay Nodine ~

Winner D37 Humorous Contest 2007

With age comes wisdom.
With wisdom comes the Golden Years.
With the Golden Years
Comes Hardees 99-cent biscuits—
And—Senior—Discount—Coffee.

Mr. Contest Master, fellow Toastmasters and Guests—
I'm not knocking Senior Citizen discounts, mind you
For when you reach the Golden Years
Every penny counts!
Plus—I live for the Senior Citizen—Early Bird Special
Of HA-BA-NERO pepper-crusted trout
At McCabe's Restaurant—every Friday afternoon.

However—each time I find a place
That offers a Senior Citizen Discount
I find a bunch of people in their Golden Years
Telling the person next to them—Oh—
"I'm on a fixed income!"
"I'm on a fixed income."

Well—I want you to know
That is not true in my case——
I am on a declining income!!!!——
And the only thing golden about the Golden Years
Is the gold I transfer from my bank account
To the medical profession.

Now—It seems like only yesterday—
But it MUST have been a Friday
Because I picked up my Senior Citizen—Early Bird Special
Of Habanero pepper-crusted trout
At McCabe's on my way home.

Before that—
I was sitting in my doctor's office
Complaining about—

- Shortness of breath
- Loss of stamina
- And numbness in the arms

He was saying
"All the tests looked normal
But I'm thinking it could be the heart.
We need to run a few tests.
In the meantime—
I am prescribing these pills that are expensive
And may have some side effects."
Side effects!!!
I wasn't worried about my sides—It was

- Shortness of breath
- Loss of stamina
- And numbness in the arms

That I worried about.

Now—It seems like only yesterday—
But it MUST have been a Friday
Since I barely made the Senior Citizen—Early Bird Special
Of Habanero pepper-crusted trout—at McCabe's.

There I was
At the Heart Center
Taking stress tests—
CAT Scans—EKGs—MRIs.
After the tests, the doctor said
Everything looks normal
And that I had a strong, healthy heart.
However—I am sending you to a specialist in Charlotte
In the meantime—take the pills I am prescribing.
They are very expensive—
And may have some very serious side effects! <Waist gestures>

Now—It seems like only yesterday

Speeches to Learn From

But there I was—on a Friday
At the Presbyterian Hospital
On the examination table
Worried about missing
My Senior Citizen—Early Bird Special
Of Habanero pepper-crusted trout.

I was heavily sedated
When I heard this far away voice—
Mr. Nodine—Mr. Nodine—can you hear me?
Yes!
Again—the voice—
Sir—we are going to take this sharp probe
Put it into your groin
Push it up to your heart
So we can run a test.
I said—OK!

As it turned out—
Diagnosis—the same!!!
The heart appears strong and healthy
The doctor was telling me again.
I'm going to prescribe these pills that are very expensive.
(I know, I know—they may have side effects.)
No—but they will enhance the symptoms you have now.

Now, it seems like only yesterday,
But it must have been—
No, I'm sure it was—yesterday.
I got a call from the Heart Center
at North-east Medical Center.
They told me to come by their office
They wanted to discuss my case further.

As I was pulling into the North-east Medical Parking deck,
There was a sign that read—SPEED LIMIT—5 mph.
You can't drive 5 mph.!!!
When you start your car—
What are you doing—7 ????

Well—you guessed it.

I was stopped for speeding
Pulled over by the Security Police.
He wasn't in a car—
He was just walking along beside me.

A big burly fellow with those mirrored sunglasses.
Leaning over and looking into my car—
Buddy—do you have any idea
How fast you were going? he asked.
I don't know—maybe 6.

Without changing expression—he said
We have you on radar—you were going 9 !!!!
Nine!!!!—
No way, I said,
My front-end shimmies at 8!

As I was lamenting over the $90 ticket
The doctor was saying
Mr. Nodine your heart seems to be in good shape—
But you are taking far too many pills.
He also said—
We have had over a hundred people this month
With the same symptoms as you—
We have traced it to McCabe's Restaurant.
We have discovered—that habanero pepper and fish oil
Will cause—

- Shortness of breath
- Loss of stamina
- And numbness in the arms

SO YOU ARE SAYING
NOTHING IS WRONG WITH MY HEART???
Mr. Nodine, I can safely say
Your heart will last—as long as you do!!!

Well then, I asked—
DO YOU THINK I WILL LIVE TO BE 80?
He asked—do you smoke or drink in excess?

Oh no, I said.
He asked—do you eat red meat?
I shook my head, noooo.
He asked—do you drive fast cars—and chase loose women?
No, I said—I DON'T DO ANY OF THOSE THINGS.
He said————
THEN—WHY DO YOU CARE?

... Mr Toastmaster

Jay Nodine, DTM, was a member of the Goldmine Club in NC (District 37) for decades. He also served as a Board member of Toastmasters International®. Jay, always warm and funny, won D37's Humorous Speech Contest in four consecutive years—a record. This was one of those speeches.

Tribute to a Dog
~ George Graham Vest ~
September 23, 1870

Vest represented a client whose hunting dog, a foxhound named Drum (or Old Drum), had been killed by a sheep farmer. The dog's owner was suing for damages in the amount of $50, the maximum allowed by law. During the trial, Vest stated that he would "win the case or apologize to every dog in Missouri." His closing argument to the jury made no reference to any of the testimony previously offered during the trial. Instead, he closed this way:

Gentlemen of the Jury—
The best friend a man has in the world
May turn against him
And become his enemy.
His son or daughter
That he has reared with loving care
May prove ungrateful.
Those who are nearest and dearest to us
Those whom we trust
With our happiness and our good name
May become traitors to their faith.
The money that a man has—he may lose.
It flies away from him,
Perhaps when he needs it most.
A man's reputation
May be sacrificed
In a moment of ill-considered action.
The people
Who are prone to fall on their knees
To do us honor
When success is with us
May be the first
To throw the stone of malice
When failure settles its cloud upon our heads.

The one absolutely unselfish friend
That man can have in this selfish world—
The one that never deserts him
The one that never proves ungrateful
Or treacherous
Is his dog.

A man's dog stands by him
In prosperity and in poverty,
In health and in sickness.
He will sleep on the cold ground,
Where the wintry winds blow
And the snow drives fiercely,
If only he may be near his master's side.
He will kiss the hand
That has no food to offer.
He will lick the wounds and sores
That come in encounters
With the roughness of the world.
He guards the sleep of his pauper master
As if he were a prince.
When all other friends desert—
He remains.
When riches take wings
And reputation falls to pieces
He is as constant in his love
As the sun in its journey through the heavens.

If fortune drives the master forth
An outcast in the world
Friendless and homeless
The faithful dog asks no higher privilege
Than that of accompanying him
To guard him against danger
To fight against his enemies.

And when the last scene of all comes
And death takes his master in its embrace
And his body is laid away in the cold ground
No matter if all other friends pursue their way
There by the graveside will the noble dog be found
His head between his paws
His eyes sad
But open in alert watchfulness
Faithful and true
Even in death.

Vest won the case. A statue of the dog stands in front of the Warrensburg, Missouri, courthouse.

The Whiskey Speech
Delivered to Mississippi State Legislators
~ Rep. Noah S. "Soggy" Sweat, Jr ~
April 4, 1952

The speech concerned the question of the prohibition of alcoholic liquor,
a law then in force in Mississippi

My friends
I had not intended
To discuss this controversial subject
At this particular time.

However—I want you to know
That I do not shun controversy—
On the contrary
I will take a stand on any issue—At any time—
Regardless of how fraught with controversy
It might be.

You have asked me—
How I feel about whiskey.
All right—Here is how I feel about whiskey.

If—when you say whiskey—
You mean—
The devil's brew
The poison scourge
The bloody monster
That defiles innocence
Dethrones reason
Destroys the home
Creates misery—and poverty—
Yea—literally takes the bread
From the mouths of little children.

If you mean —the evil drink
That topples the Christian man and woman
From the pinnacle of righteous, gracious living
Into the bottomless pit of degradation—
And despair—and shame—
And helplessness—and hopelessness
Then—certainly—I am against it.

But if—when you say whiskey—
You mean the oil of conversation
The philosophic wine—
The ale that is consumed
When good fellows get together—
That puts a song in their hearts
And laughter on their lips
And the warm glow of contentment
In their eyes—
If you mean Christmas cheer
If you mean the stimulating drink
That puts the spring in the old gentleman's step
On a frosty, crispy morning
If you mean the drink
Which enables a man to magnify his joy
And his happiness
And to forget—If only for a little while—
Life's great tragedies
And heartaches—and sorrows

If you mean that drink—
The sale of which pours into our treasuries
Untold millions of dollars
Which are used to provide tender care
For our little crippled children
Our blind—our deaf—our dumb
Our pitiful aged—and infirm
To build highways
And hospitals
And schools
Then—certainly—I am for it!

This is my stand.
I will not retreat from it.
I will not compromise.

This speech is renowned for the way in which it seems to come down firmly and decisively on both sides of the question. The speech gave rise to the phrase If-by-whiskey, used to illustrate such equivocation in argument.

Source: Wikipedia

Speaker Superscripts

World Speech Champions (WCPS or WSC)

[74] 1974 WSC Bennie Powell
[75] 1975 WSC Andy McKay
[76] 1976 WSC William Johnson
[77] 1977 WSC Evelyn Jane Burgay
[78] 1978 WSC Michael Aun II
[79] 1979 WSC Dick Caldwell
[80] 1980 WSC Jeff Young
[81] 1981 WSC Jim Joelson
[82] 1982 WSC Kenneth Bernard
[83] 1983 WSC Roy Fenstermaker
[84] 1984 WSC Joe Boyd
[85] 1985 WSC Marie C. Pyne
[86] 1986 WSC Arabella Bengson
[87] 1987 WSC Harold Patterson
[88] 1988 WSC Jerry Starke
[89] 1989 WSC Don Johnson
[90] 1990 WSC David Brooks
[91] 1991 WSC David Ross
[92] 1992 WSC Dana LaMon
[93] 1993 WSC Otis Williams Jr
[94] 1994 WSC Morgan McArthur
[95] 1995 WSC Mark Brown
[96] 1996 WSC David Nottage
[97] 1997 WSC Willie Jones
[98] 1998 WSC Brett Rutledge
[99] 1999 WSC Craig Valentine
[00] 2000 WSC Ed Tate
[01] 2001 WSC Darren LaCroix
[02] 2002 WSC Wayne Smith
[03] 2003 WSC Jim Key
[04] 2004 WSC Randy Harvey
[05] 2005 WSC Lance Miller
[06] 2006 WSC Edward Hearn
[07] 2007 WSC Vikas Jhingran
[08] 2008 WSC LaShunda Rundles
[09] 2009 WSC Mark Hunter
[10] 2010 WSC David Henderson
[11] 2011 WSC Jock Elliott
[12] 2012 WSC Ryan Avery
[13] 2013 WSC Presiyan Vasilev
[14] 2014 WSC Dananjaya Hettiarachchi
[15] 2015 WSC Mohammed Qahtani
[16] 2016 WSC Darren Tay Wen Jie

WSC 2nd and 3rd Place Winners Quoted
[Year and Place]

[74-3] Joel Weldon
[79-3] Ted Mathew
[94-2] Hans Lillejord
[94-3] Jock Elliott
[95-2] Phillip Khan-Panni
[96-2] Jana Barnhill
[96-3] Frank Morris
[97-2] Evelyn Peyton
[98-3] Robert Ferguson
[99-2] Albert Mensah
[01-2] Jim Key
[01-3] J A Gamache
[02-2] Jim Key
[02-3] Jonah Mungoshi
[03-2] David Sanfacon
[04-2] Douglas Kroger
[04-3] James Webb
[05-2] Angela Louie
[06-2] Douglas Wilson
[06-3] Rich Hopkins
[08-2] Loghandran Krishnasamy
[08-3] Katherine Morrison
[09-3] Erick Rainey
[10-2] Robert Mackenzie
[10-3] Linus Chang
[11-2] Kwong Yue Yang
[12-2] Palaniappa Subramaniam
[12-3] Stuart Pink
[13-2] Kingi Biddle
[13-3] Shurooq AlBanna
[14-2] Kwong Yue Yang
[14-3] Kelly Sergent
[15-2] Aditya Maheswaran
[15-3] Manoj Vasudevan
[16-2] Aaron Beverly

Other WSC Finalists Quoted
[Year and Finalist's Initials]

91-PH	Peter Hempenstall
93-RS	Richard Spencer
97-JB	Jeremiah Bacon
97-SZ	Sandra Ziegler
98-RB	Rick Brunton
99-JE	Julie Esguerra
00-MH	Mark Haugh
01-EP	Evelyn Peyton
01-LL	Larry Lands
02-CW	Craig Weathers
03-BW	Brian Woolf
03-JM	Jason Malham
03-JS	Jeannine Scott
06-JE	Jock Elliott
06-MA	Mohammed Ali
06-RV	Rory Vaden
06-TL	Thomas Lindaman
07-BP	Bryant Pergerson
07-DK	Douglas Kruger
07-RK	Robert Killen
09-CN	Chakisse Newton
09-MZ	Maureen Zappala
10-IH	Ian Humphrey
11-KB	Kingi Biddle
11-OR	Oscar Rivas
12-DP	Diane Parker
12-KRM	Kenny Ray Morgan
12-ML	Mario Lewis
13-JW	Jon White
14-SD	Sharook Darawala
15-EF	Eric Feinendegen
15-GM	Gil Michelini
15-JJ	James Jeffley
15-PH	Patrick Hammond
15-RD	Russ Dantu
16-KH	Katina Hunter

WSC Quotes From Semi-Finalists
[Year of Semi-Final and Initials]

02DS	Dwayne Smith
03BW	Brian Woolf
04RH	Randy Harvey
05LM	Lance Miller
06DW	Douglas Wilson
06RH	Rich Hopkins
07VJ	Vikas Jhingran
10CR	Christine Robinson
10DH	David Henderson
10DP	Dwight Pledger
10JA	Jonathan Abuyan
10JG	Joseph Grondin
10JM	Josef Martens
10KYY	Kwong Yue Yang
10LC	Linus Chang
10MD	Michael Desidero
10PH	Patricia Hill
10RD	Russ Dantu
10RG	Robin Grieve
11AT	Anne Michelle Taylor
13RS	Ray Schnell
14CA	Charles Austin
15BT	Byron Taylor
15DW	Diana Watson
15EB	Eric Beba
15EF	Eric Feinendegen
15GA	Geneva Anderson
15JJ	James Jeffley
15JO	Johan Ooi Keng Kee
15KM	Kory May
15LF	Linda Forde
15MA	Mike Anthony
15MQ	Mohammed Qahtani
15PH	Patrick Hammond
15WK	William Knight
15WP	William Powell
16DB	Daach'ana Blaydes
16DT	Darren Tay Wen Jie
16EE	Elliott Eddy
16KH	Katina Hunter
16JL	Josephine Lee
16RM	Richard Madison
16SJ	Sherwood Jones
16SS	Simon Scriver

Other References
[Differentiating Initials]

AB.	Alison Boyce
ACC	Arthur C Clarke
AD.	April Dunn
AD^	Andy Dooley
AE	Albert Einstein
AL	Abraham Lincoln
AL.	Allen Ladd
AM	Ashley Montagu
AP	Alan S Paton
AS	Adlai Stevenson
B	Bible
BB	Bob Buford
BB.	Bob Boylan
BC	Bill Clinton
BF	Ben Franklin
BJ	Barbara Jordan
BM	Bill Mintz
BO	Barack Obama
BR	Bob Richards
BT	Buddhist Tradition
BT+	Barbara Tuchman
BW	Billy Wilder
BW.	Brian Woolf
CA.	Charlie Anderson
CB	Carl Bard
CM	Christopher Myers
CM+	Charles Malik
CNB	Christian Nestell Bovee
CR	Cavett Robert [42]
CS	Chief Seattle
CV	Craig Valentine [99]
DB	David Brooks [90]
DB^	Dave Barry
DD.	Deborah Davis
DL	Darren LaCroix [01]
DOI	Declaration of Independence
DA	Douglas MacArthur
DR	Dave Ramsey
DS	Doug Stevenson
DW	Dan Weedin
DW.	Douglas Wilson
E	Euripides
EBW	E. B. White
ECS	Elizabeth Cady Stanton
EH	Eric Hoffer
EH.	Ed Hearn
EK	Edward Kennedy

EM	Edward R. Murrow
EN	Earl Nightingale
ER	Eleanor Roosevelt
ET	Ed Tate [00]
EW	Eric Woolson
EW^	Emlyn Williams
FB	Francis Bacon
FD	Frederick Douglass
FDR	Franklin D. Roosevelt
GA.	Geneva Anderson
GF	Gerald Ford
GGV	George Gentry Vest
GS	Gloria Steinem
GV	Gore Vidal
HEF	Harry Emerson Fosdick
HM	Hugh McLeod
IC	Irvin Cobb
JAG.	J A Gamache
JB.	Jana Barnhill
JB	Jimmy Buffett
JC	Johnny Cochran
JC^	Julius Caesar
JCH	James C. Humes
JFK	John F. Kennedy
JG	James D. Griffin
JJ	Jesse Jackson
JJ.	Jane Jude
JK	Jim Key [03]
JM	Jon Morrow
JN.	Jay Nodine
JS	John Steinbeck
JT	Justin Trudeau
JW	Sen. Jim Webb
JW^	Joel Weldon
JW+	John Whitehead
KA	Kofi Annan
KB	Karl Barth
KC	Prof. Karen Chase
KC.	Kirk Carr
KM	Kweisi Mfume
KM.	Kevin McCue
KP	Kathleen Parker
KS.	Ken Sloan
KT	Kevin Taylor
LB	Les Brown
LBJ	Lyndon B. Johnson
LC	Lee Child
LG	Sen. Lindsey Graham
LM	Lance Miller [05]
LM^	Lisa Martin

LN	Liam Napier	RWE	Ralph Waldo Emerson
MA	Mike Atkin	SBA	Susan B Anthony
MA^	Michael Aun [78]	SG	Sumantra Ghoshal
MAL	Mary Ann Lipscomb	SH	Steve Hansen
MB	Mark Brown [95]	SL^	Sam Leith
MC	Mario Cuomo	SL	Susan Lamb
MD	Maureen Dowd	SN.	Sarfaraz Nazir
MF	Mary Fisher	SS	Steve Siemens
MJ.	Mary Joseph	STC	Samuel Taylor Coleridge
MM	Sen. Mike Mansfield	SW	Steven Wright
MMc	Morgan McArthur [94]	TB	The Beatles
MP	Max De Pree	TB+	Ty Boyd
MP^	Mathieu Pigasse	TC	Terry Canfield
MR	Mitt Romney	TC.	Todd Collins
MR^	Mandrallius Robinson	TC^	Ted Cruz
MT	Mark Twain	TF	Tom Friedman
MT.	Minnie Thomas	TG	Tex Guinan
MVH	Mark Victor Hansen	TI	Toastmasters International®
MW	Mae West	TR	Tony Robbins
N	News	TR^	Theodore Roosevelt
NF	Niall Ferguson	VJ	Vikas Jhingran [07]
NK	Neil Kinnock	W	Wikipedia
NM	Nelson Mandela	WA	Woody Allen
NP	Neil Postman	WC	Winston Churchill
NS	Noah Sweat	WD^	Wayne Dwyer
OW	Otis Williams Jr [93]	WD+	Will Durant
PF	Patricia Fripp	WI	Washington Irving
PKP	Phillip Kahn-Panni	WJB	William Jennings Bryan
PO	P J O'Rourke	WLP	William Lyon Phelps
PS	Paul Shane Spear	WM.	Will May
PV	Presiyan Vasilev [13]	WS	William Shakespeare
RA	Ryan Avery [12]	YB	Yogi Berra
RC.	Ron Chapman	ZMB	Zanny Minton Beddoes
RD.	Russ Dantu	ZZ	Zig Ziglar
RE	Sir Rod Eddington		
RF	Robert Frost		
RF^	Roy Fenstermaker [83]		
RH	Randy Harvey [04]		
RH^	Rich Hopkins		
RM.	Rusty Mitchell		
RM.^	Rico McDaniel		
RN	Richard Nixon		
RPC	Roy Peter Clark		
RR	Ronald Reagan		
RR.	Rebecca Raglan		
RS	Robert Schuler		
RS.	Richard Spencer		
RT	Ross Turner		
RW	Rick Warren		
RW.	Ruth Witty		

Abbreviations & General Notes

Abbreviations Used

TI   Toastmasters International®

WCPS   Toastmasters World Championship of Public Speaking® (The Annual Contest)
           World Champion of Public Speaking (The Winner of the Annual Contest)

WSC   Toastmasters World Championship of Public Speaking® (The Annual Contest)
           World Speaking Champion (Winner of the Annual Contest)

Recommended Books as Core Companions for any Speaker

B1   *Story Theater Method* by Doug Stevenson

B2   *Speak Like Churchill, Stand Like Lincoln* by James C. Humes

B3   *Speaker Leader Champion* by Jeremy Donovan and Ryan Avery
     [This book includes the full text of 11 WSC Speeches]

B4   *The Elements of Excellence* by Mark Forsyth
     [This delightfully written book gives the rhetorical terms of the tools used in this
     book and offers many additional elements.]

Recommended Websites

www.billspro.com/toastmasters – Offers WCPS speeches through 2011 [Fee-based]

www.toastmastersondemand.com – Offers WCPS contests from 2012 [Fee-based]

www.ted.com – Offers excellent video presentations on diverse subjects [Free]

http://sixminutes.dlugan.com – Offers a range of helpful speech information.

Websites to learn about Toastmasters International®

www.toastmasters.org

www.toastmasters.org/Find-a-Club

Interested in Further Exploration of Some of the Terms Used?

Search Google for these rhetorical terms related to the tools:

Contrast	Antithesis
Exaggeration	Hyperbole
Parallelism	Parallelism, Hendiatris, Tricolon
Repetition	Anaphora, Epiphora, Anadiplosis, Chiasmus, Epanados
Rhyme	Assonance

About the Author

Brian Woolf is a speechaholic. He loves listening to speeches, thinking about them, and giving them; and he loves reading and studying them—their makeup, their message, their music—to discover their magic.

It wasn't always so. In high school he ardently avoided entering the annual speech contests. While at University he "bombed" with a speech at a major black-tie dinner. At 22, in his first job, he knew he needed speaking help. Toastmasters clubs were just being introduced to his native New Zealand. He joined. He learned. He gained speaking confidence ... enough to subsequently use the skills learned to graduate with Distinction from Harvard Business School with its two-year program of dialog-based case studies. In later years, he has spoken extensively, including to conferences on five continents.

Toastmasters' plays a key part in his life. Brian has been an active member in clubs in New Zealand, Ireland, and six States in the USA. Besides earning its highest award, Distinguished Toastmaster (DTM), he has won six District (State) Speech Contests—and lost many more (which is when intensive learning occurs!) In 2003, he was one of nine finalists in Toastmasters World Championship of Public Speaking®.

Mastering communication skills helped him not only at Toastmasters but also in the business world and as an author, where the art of simple, clear communication guided his writing of three marketing books.

In this book, Brian shares many of the lessons he wishes he had learned decades ago with the hope that it will speed up your speaking journey.

Comments and suggestions

Should you wish to share any comments or suggestions, or have any quotations you think worthy of inclusion in a future reprint or a posting on our website, please send them to: *brianwoolf@speakers-toolbox.com*

For more information

Visit our website: *www.speakers-toolbox.com*

Made in the USA
Middletown, DE
08 February 2019